I Just Want to be Loved

CASEY WATSON

THE *SUNDAY TIMES* BESTSELLING AUTHOR

I Just Want to be Loved

Abandoned and alone, she has nothing else to lose

This book is a work of non-fiction based on the author's experiences.
In order to protect privacy, names, identifying characteristics,
dialogue and details have been changed or reconstructed.

HarperElement
An imprint of HarperCollins*Publishers*
1 London Bridge Street
London SE1 9GF

www.harpercollins.co.uk

HarperCollins*Publishers*
1st Floor, Watermarque Building, Ringsend Road
Dublin 4, Ireland

First published by HarperElement 2022

1 3 5 7 9 10 8 6 4 2

© Casey Watson 2022

Casey Watson asserts the moral right to
be identified as the author of this work

A catalogue record of this book is
available from the British Library

PB ISBN 9780008484859
EB ISBN 9780008484866

Printed and bound in the UK using 100%
renewable electricity at CPI Group (UK) Ltd

MIX
Paper from
responsible sources

FSC
www.fsc.org
FSC™ C007454

This book is produced from independently certified FSC™ paper
to ensure responsible forest management.

For more information visit: www.harpercollins.co.uk/green

Dedication

What a year it's been! We are all now living in our new normal and it often feels like things will never be the same again. Work, travel, leisure time and even seeing our loved ones now carry certain risks and life can be pretty scary. There are things that have changed for the better too. Our time has suddenly become more important to us, our loved ones more precious. We have learned to develop relationships in new and unique ways and life online has never been so popular. In fact, I'd like to thank a particularly lovely online friend, Marc Alan Powers Egan, and dedicate this book to him. Despite the problems that a chronic illness presents him with, he has tirelessly devoted his precious time to running a Facebook group targeted to readers of memoirs – Fostering Memoirs and Fiction Book Club. He promotes lots of lovely authors on there, including myself, sharing his enthusiasm for life and interacting regularly with all of the members and authors.

Acknowledgements

Firstly I want to thank my fabulous agent, Andrew Lownie, and the wonderful team at HarperCollins, who continue to do such an amazing job. Ten years and counting now ... wow. Plus special thanks to Holly Blood, who has taken over the reins. Will be great when we can finally meet in person!

As always, I need to thank my beautiful friend Lynne Barrett-Lee, who takes my work and helps to transform it into the stories my readers love. We've been a team for many years now, and Lynne is a much-valued friend.

I pay tribute to my lovely family, my husband and my close friends, who patiently listen to me rant on about the trials and tribulations of being a foster carer. Always there to give me fabulous advice and quick to point out all the positives when I feel things are going badly.

And lastly the most important people of all, you, my readers. If it weren't for you, my stories simply wouldn't

Casey Watson

be out there. The wonderful reviews you leave me have really kept my spirits up this year and I'm so, so thankful. As always, I send my love to you all.

Chapter 1

I was very excited. As in very, very, *very* excited. Excited in a way that I hadn't been excited since … well, probably ever. Not this kind of excited, in any case. So, I had barely got in through the front door before I was shouting ideas over my shoulder, to Mike, who was following me up the path.

'I'm going to have to think about my outfit,' I was saying, as he came in behind me. 'I mean, given the time of year do you think a suit might be best? I mean, I know it's not really me, but what do you think? I don't want to be freezing my proverbials off, do I? And you too. God, the only one that fits you would have the fashion police around in seconds! Mind you, perhaps Keiron's thinking we'll go posh. Have you all matching. I should have asked him. I'll have to call him …'

Mike rolled his eyes, no doubt realising that this 'planning' (he'd call it 'mania') would go on for many months to come. I didn't care, though. It wasn't every day that your son and his fiancée took you out for lunch to announce they were getting married, was it?

'Oh, I do hope they manage to get a Christmas date booked,' I enthused. I was already picturing the scene. Like that one in the *Bridget Jones* movie. 'Everywhere dusted in white,' I rattled on at Mike, 'snowflakes still gently falling, the bride and her bridesmaids wearing white, faux-fur capes, with matching mufflers, and dainty gloves, and ...'

'It's *May*,' Mike pointed out. 'Take a breath, love, for goodness' sake. They've only just bloody told us. And I don't think they'll appreciate you diving straight in with all your mad ideas, either. At least not *just* yet,' he added, his expression softening now, on seeing mine a little crestfallen. 'Put the kettle on, will you? I think we've had quite enough excitement for one day.'

Party pooper, I thought, as I went into the kitchen. But no matter. In a bit, I could get on the phone to Riley. She'd been minding Kieron and Lauren's youngest (it hardly seemed possible that little Carter was almost nine months old now) so that Kieron and Lauren could take us out and treat us, and I knew she'd be as keen to do some wedding chat as I was, so I could pick up where I'd left off soon enough. And men just didn't get it – well, the men of my acquaintance, at any rate. It took *months* to plan a wedding properly. Everyone knew that. So, the time to start was now, whether Mike wanted to get involved or not.

I Just Want to be Loved

To be fair, that 'or not' was probably a given. And not just because my husband had no interest in bridal fashion (or any fashion, come to that), but because he wasn't generally a 'looking forward to it' kind of man. He preferred enjoying the here and now, especially now we were both of us into our mid-fifties and time seemed to be whooshing past ever faster. And it had been a pretty intense start to the year, to be fair; up until three weeks ago we'd barely had time to draw breath, owing to the mother and baby placement we'd taken on back in January. And though we'd fallen in love with little Seth and Tommy and, indeed, their mummy, Jenna, it had been the kind of placement that couldn't help but take a huge physical toll on us, as well as the emotional one, as life with tiny people in the house can't help but do.

So, we'd taken a break, a proper break (Mike even took three weeks off work), starting with a week in Fuerteventura, just the two of us in the balmy heat, eating and drinking cocktails, and doing nothing very much at all, bar languid swims and sitting watching the glorious sunsets. We'd followed that with a couple of weeks just enjoying what had come to feel like a real novelty – having nothing to worry about other than what time to drag ourselves out of bed in the morning.

But I can only spend so much time doing nothing very much, so Mike's return to work after the weekend would mean a return for me too; I'd already told Christine Bolton, my supervising social worker, to make

3

a note that I was going into full-on spring-clean mode and would be ready to return to the fostering coal face at the beginning of June.

But that was still almost a fortnight away, so when my phone chirruped to say that a message had arrived, I was surprised to see her name on the display. 'I wonder what she wants,' I said to Mike as he spooned coffee into our mugs.

'So, look at the message,' he answered. 'That's like going to the front door and saying, "I wonder who it is."'

'Oh, be quiet,' I huffed at him, squinting to see what it said, which was: *I know you're still on leave but can you call me? I need someone to do a week's respite. Would be really grateful.*

'Hmm. Do I want to do a week's respite?' I asked Mike.

He shrugged. 'Up to you, love. I'm back at work Monday, so if you think you're ready for another one, go for it. It'll give you something to do while Tyler's away, won't it?'

Like I didn't already have enough to do with a Christmas wedding to plan? But he was right. Tyler, our son, whom we'd fostered since he was eleven, had just taken himself off for ten days with his girlfriend, Naomi – a road trip to York, to use up some of the annual leave they'd both amassed at work and, in part, so they could spend a few days in the city where, come September, she'd be starting at university.

4

About which I was obviously fretting. What would happen come September when that day came around, and they'd be separated by some hundred-odd miles? Because if I knew one thing, it was that the relationship was getting serious. So, it would be a difficult wrench for them both.

But there was nothing I could do. They would have to work that out for themselves. And Mike was right. A respite placement would be a welcome distraction from worrying about things I had no control over. 'You're right,' I agreed as I scrolled through to Christine's number. It would also be a good way to break me back in. And possibly an even better way of ensuring I didn't go *too* mad on the wedding preparation front. I wasn't perfect, by any means, but one thing I did pride myself on was self-knowledge; I knew what I was like. Which, when it came to planning exciting family events, was like a bull at a gate. I should heed Mike's advice and rein myself in a little.

'*Yes!*' Christine said immediately. 'I was praying you'd get back to me. I half thought that you might have jetted off somewhere again, making the most of it while you still had the chance.'

'No such luck,' I said. 'Mike has to be back at work next week, sadly.' And, in truth, I missed the grandkids too much to be away from them for more than a week or so, anyway, but that wasn't the kind of thing I would generally share with Christine. She'd lost her only child to cot death, and had never had another, so I was always mindful of the kind of joys that were so cruelly denied her. 'So, about this favour,' I said instead. 'What have you got for me?'

'Just a week's respite,' Christine said, 'for a fourteen-year-old girl, Elise Blackwell. She only moved to our area nine months ago and has been fostered for the last few weeks with Jan Howard. I think you already know Jan?' I did. And I liked her. She was great fun to be around and also an experienced carer. We'd hit it off immediately the first time we'd met and had palled up at various training sessions over the years. 'Well,' Christine continued. 'Jan's holiday has been booked for ages. And Marie Jackson and her husband were all set to do the respite, but yesterday poor Marie was in a nasty car accident. She's not seriously injured, but looking after kids is definitely off the cards for a while. Her hubby works away from home too, so he can't step in, and that's when I thought of you and Mike. Is it something you think you could do for us?'

I didn't really need to think, because it sounded so straightforward. 'Of course we can,' I said, glancing at Mike, already knowing I didn't have to run this one by him. 'Is it imminent or will we get to meet the girl first?'

'If you desperately wanted to meet first, I can't see a problem, but the respite is from Monday, so ...'

'Don't worry, then,' I told her. 'But some background would be helpful. I mean, I know it's only a week, but forewarned is forearmed. Is there anything in particular I should know about beforehand?'

Christine understood, of course, and she also knew that I was a bit of a stickler for gathering intel, because the smallest thing could sometimes cause the biggest fuss. I'd learned that the hard way, right at the start of my fostering journey, when I'd done a week's emergency care for a seven-year-old. Like so many of my placements, the call had come in late at night from the Emergency Duty Team. The child had been left home alone by her mother for two days and had only gone to a neighbour for help when the food had run out. I'd agreed to a short placement while her grandparents were assessed urgently, and had quickly made up a bed using a princess-themed duvet cover and pillowcases. The poor girl, who'd been obviously distraught when she'd arrived, had a complete meltdown when we tried to put her to bed. It turned out that the mother's boyfriend had been sexually abusing her, and his name for her was Uncle Darren's little princess. I vowed never to make a mistake like that again. At least, not if I could do anything to prevent it.

'Well, considering Elise was only picked up by our authority less than a year ago,' Christine said, 'she has a file the size of a metaphorical phone book. But I'll try to give you a brief rundown of her background.'

She went on to explain that the girl had lived all over the place, first with Dad, then with Mum, then later with her paternal grandmother, and a whole host of other places besides, since that time, including sofa surfing with various friends.

'In fact, that's how she first came to our attention,' Christine explained. 'She'd been staying with one friend whose mother became concerned that Elise didn't seem to be attending school, and, more worryingly, that neither did she appear to have anywhere to call home. Thankfully, she was worried enough to call us. So, we did some digging and it turned out that though Elise was meant to be living with her paternal grandmother at that time – Mrs Blackwell – she hardly ever stayed there. And when we went to check *her* out, she refused to have Elise back. Mrs Blackwell – Grandma – said she was too old to be looking after an out-of-control teenager, and thought it better all round if Elise went into care, not least because she had a knee replacement operation coming up in a couple of months, and, to use her words, would have more than enough on her plate without fretting about what Elise was getting up to or what time she might deign to amble home.'

'Poor kid,' I said, sighing into the phone. 'But an all too familiar story, isn't it? I'm guessing Mum and Dad refused her too, or was it that Elise wouldn't stay with them?'

Christine went on to explain that the mother had simply upped and left when Elise was just five years old, leaving Dad – already a reluctant father, apparently – to struggle alone, trying to fit in childcare with holding on to his job. This meant that Elise had been passed around various friends and family members, and sometimes left home alone for long periods, Dad clearly resenting the

8

fact that his life had been turned upside down, and the relationship between the two of them never really had a chance. Fast forward two years and Dad met a new partner, a woman who already had two children of her own. After just a few weeks the new family moved in, and Elise – clearly struggling with another huge upheaval – started playing up to get her dad's attention. Relations worsened, particularly between Elise and her new 'unofficial stepmum', and a 'her or me' stand-off ensued.

'So Dad tracked Mum down,' Christine finished, 'so he could save his new relationship. Gathered up Elise's belongings and, again, to put it simply, dumped both daughter and possessions on her mother's doorstep. Who, by now, note, had had another child. A little girl.'

Another wretchedly sad, but all too familiar story. From what I'd heard, it was clear that the girl was basically unwanted, end of. 'The poor girl,' I said again, 'and that didn't work out, either, I'm guessing.'

'You guess right,' Christine said. 'She was only with Mum for a couple of years before running away and ending up at Grandma's – the paternal grandmother, that is. Who took her in. She's been there – or mostly *not* there, ever since.'

'So, no ongoing contact with the half-sister?'

Christine shook her head. 'Or Mum, as far as we know. We do know that Dad and the paternal gran had a big falling out after Dad sent Elise packing to her mother's, and that they no longer spoke. According to the notes Gran only took Elise in because there was literally nowhere else for her to go. And guilt, of course. It wasn't ideal. She was – is – riddled with arthritis and not terribly mobile.'

I felt a familiar welling of sympathy. And anger. 'Honestly, for the life of me, I can't understand why some of these parents don't see the bloody damage they are causing,' I said to Christine. 'No, correction. They *do* see, but go right ahead and do it anyway. The poor kid. Still, at least she has Jan now. And hopefully a bit more stability ...'

'Exactly,' Christine said. 'Though she's still not back in school yet – we're working on it – so she'll be at home with you for the week. That okay?'

'Yes, of course. Probably easier than her travelling across to the other side of town anyway.'

'Oh, and one more thing,' Christine added. 'A little postscript to her pre-respite report. Just to keep in mind that Elise has been sexually active since she was around eleven, so do keep an eye on things in that department, so to speak. Just a case of following protocol, essentially, should anything arise – and there will be the usual risk assessment within her notes, so just have a good read of that when you get the chance.'

After agreeing that we'd see Elise and her social worker first thing the following Monday, I disconnected with a sense of mild unease. Though not because of Jan's note. Heaven knew, I'd fostered my share of sexually active adolescents, and for a girl with Elise's background this was hardly headline news. Sad, yes –

she'd clearly been vulnerable for her entire childhood, and it was perhaps partly why her grandmother had rejected her too. But I couldn't seem to shift the feeling that beneath the facts must be a girl in a state of profound emotional turmoil.

'More coffee?' Mike was asking, and I realised I'd already drained mine. 'And the lowdown on the girl, while I'm at it? You look like you've just been brought back down to earth with a bump.'

'Just reflecting,' I told him, as I handed him my empty mug. And mostly on the fact that so often in cases of all-out rejection by loved ones, girls could so easily go searching for love in other ways. Potentially destructive ways. Potentially dangerous ways, too. Again, tragic, but nothing unusual in it. And it wasn't my remit, I reminded myself, to worry about her future. That was Jan's department, and I didn't doubt she was doing exactly that.

I filled Mike in on the potted background Christine had told me. 'Hmm,' he said, when I'd finished. 'It never gets any easier to swallow, does it?'

I felt that way too. And perhaps things like this sticking in the throat should never change in any case. I also felt the familiar frustration with the system that so often meant us having to take children on 'blind', as in without comprehensive background notes. They would almost certainly exist, but it was, sadly, the nature of the beast that it could be a few more days before her full notes came through.

Still, this was only going to be for a week, and if I knew one thing it was this. We could deal with just a week of almost anything.

Chapter 2

By the time Monday morning had come around, I was sure that I had covered everything on my usual checklist. Bathroom gleaming, with only full bottles of shampoos, etc. on display – tick. Single bedroom aired out with freshly washed bed linen and a suitable duvet set – tick. Kitchen cupboard and fridge stocked with teenage-friendly snacks and drinks – tick. Scented candles and wax melts burning away in all the downstairs rooms – tick.

Mike had gone back to work and, for the first time since I could remember, for some reason I felt a little bit nervous about meeting my new temporary charge. I had no idea why, because this was how things had been for years, me often being the only one at home to greet social workers and a new child. There had only been a few occasions, when a child had turned up as an emergency at night or the weekend, that Mike had also been there. I gave myself a mental shake as I went to double check the conservatory. I was just being silly, I told myself sternly, as I plumped up the fluffy yellow cushions on the 'daybed' – the couch so named by eldest granddaughter, Marley Mae. She'd taken to calling it that while in the middle of claiming ownership of the whole conservatory, following the departure of the little family we'd had staying.

And not unreasonably, because it had been used as a bedroom since January, for the young mother, her newborn baby and her four-year-old. It had made more sense than trying to cram them all in upstairs, both for access to the kitchen, and the nightly small-hours bottles, and so they could have some private family space in the daytime as well.

It had worked out well, but when they left I'd had every intention of restoring it as my conservatory, not least because it was both where I liked to do my ironing, with the doors to the garden flung open, and also tuck away the laundry out of sight. At least until my forthright granddaughter (she'd just turned seven, and didn't we know it) had stepped in to argue why it should remain a spare bedroom. 'We hardly ever get to sleep over at yours, Nan,' she'd pointed out, 'and that would be the perfect space. We'd be out of the way of any foster children, but close enough so that you could keep an eye on us.'

I couldn't argue with her logic, and she was right, of course. It was only ever in between placements that the grandkids slept over, mainly because of the lack of space, so the conservatory was the ideal solution. But I hadn't reckoned on how enthusiastically she intended to transform it to suit her tastes, which currently centred around lime green and neon yellow. Within days, cupboards were scoured and local charity shops raided, and suitable throws, cushions, blankets and various knick-knacks were put in place, the net result being that I never stepped into the conservatory now without thinking I should be wearing dark glasses.

Still, it was cheerful, and the couple of sleepovers we'd had since had been lovely. Though that of course plunged me back into 'slight worry' mode, as I anticipated the arrival of my new temporary house-guest, and my odd gut feeling re-asserted itself. It would go away, I told myself, once the girl was actually with us.

Which she soon was. I was just sipping my third morning coffee when I heard the footsteps crunching along the gravel path and went to the door to greet my guests.

'Oh, hi!' I said, surprised to see a familiar face. That of Graham Baxter, a social worker I'd worked with in the past, and who'd been doing the job for something like two decades. A safe pair of hands, and a really nice man. Someone who genuinely loved, and was good at, what he did. If nothing else, this girl at least had a great team in her corner. 'Christine wasn't sure who had been allocated,' I went on, 'but it's nice to see you again, Graham.' I then smiled at the girl standing patiently by his side. 'Come on in,' I said. 'Lovely to see you, Elise. I'm Casey.'

They both followed me through to the dining area and took a seat at the table, and as I followed I caught the scent of a familiar perfume – an expensive one Riley used. Very sparingly. She only treated herself to it at airport duty frees after their annual holiday. But perhaps I was wrong. It could equally have been one of those cheap copies you could buy on the internet.

But perhaps not, given the undoubtedly genuine designer handbag the girl was now placing on the dining-room table. She smiled shyly at me as she did so, then at Graham. 'Yup,' she simpered at him. 'Poor old Graham drew the short straw.'

'Hey, less of the old!' he quipped, and I obviously smiled politely, but was I imagining it or was there a slight tension there? The power dynamic ever so slightly out of place?

I dismissed the thought. Kids often tried to tease and 'play' their social workers. Test the boundaries of what was and wasn't acceptable. It was all part of the bigger picture when it came to kids with troubled backgrounds and, given the complicated nature of being in care, it wasn't exactly unexpected – they were having to negoti-ate new relationships with strangers who were *in loco parentis*, after all.

'Well, if Graham is old,' I said, 'that makes me Methuselah, pretty much. Anyway, it's lovely to meet you. And even lovelier that you've brought the sunshine with you too. I think the forecast is good all week, as well. Anyway, sit down, both, and I'll go grab some coffees. Or tea? Or a soft drink, perhaps, Elise?'

'I'm good,' she said. 'Graham treated me to a caramel macchiato on the way over here, didn't you? And deee-*licious* it was too.' And once again, she trained her gaze on him – a gaze under which he didn't seem entirely comfortable. But then, the whole package was arresting, no question. Elise was clearly an intelligent, articulate girl, and clearly very comfortable in her skin. She also had quite a posh accent, I noted, and I wondered what part of the country she'd picked that up from, or whether her parents were well-to-do. She was also, to use a hackneyed phrase, drop-dead gorgeous. Long blonde hair that had been artfully styled to look as if the tumbling waves in it were natural, manicured nails, contoured cheeks, barely there lash extensions, and the kind of heavy, defined brows that were currently all the rage. The thought crossed my mind that poor Jan, her regular carer, must have to pay out a fortune to keep this girl in tip-top condition.

Since Graham didn't want anything either, I joined them at the table. 'Lovely outfit,' I said, checking out the stylishly ripped skinny jeans, topped with a gleaming white T-shirt and finished with flat gold sandals. I was happy about the flats – she already towered over me! (A not-uncommon experience, but still ...)

'Thanks,' she said, accepting the compliment with a flick of her hair. 'Jan bought me the whole outfit,

17

specially to come here. The jeans are cool, aren't they? How old do you think I look?'

I felt thrown by the question. It seemed such an odd thing to ask me. Was she hoping I'd say eighteen? Because, with the make-up and the height, that was how old she *did* look. Before the advent of scrupulous ID inspections (and thank goodness for them, frankly), she'd have been able to buy alcohol in every pub for miles. But I felt strangely reluctant to play the game with her. 'Oh, it's no use asking me,' I said. 'I'm hopeless at guessing ages. Plus, I already know yours, so I wouldn't be guessing anyway. But lovely. You look lovely. Anyway, we –'

'Thanks,' she said again, her mouth widening in a mega-watt smile that practically lit up the dining room. 'I could show you how to do your own make-up one day if you like. I've been learning how to do professional makeovers and I'm getting really good at it. Specially contouring. I do tutorials on YouTube,' she added, while unashamedly scrutinising my currently blank facial canvas, presumably seeing much work to be done there.

I didn't miss Graham's reddening face as he shuffled his paperwork around. He cleared his throat. 'We'd best sort out all the boring stuff,' he said. 'I need to be on my way in about ten minutes. Got a visit to do on the way back to the office. Shall we crack on now?' he added, glancing at Elise pointedly.

As I listened to Graham reel off all the usual titles for the pieces of paper that made up a care plan, the only impression I could fix on about the girl who sat across the table was that she really didn't seem to have a care in the world. Well, not beyond the precise shape of her perfectly arched eyebrows. That odd comment about her age aside, she seemed relaxed and full of confidence. Not in the forced way some children affected as a line of best defence, but genuinely relaxed in her skin. If it *was* a mask she was making a good job of it. Yet I also realised I might have to revise my knee-jerk reaction to having heard her story from Christine. Perhaps she was more emotionally resilient than I'd anticipated. Perhaps there was more to know about her relationship with her grandmother, too. For all that they had apparently been at loggerheads in recent months, maybe her bond with her gran was a strong one and might even endure, if, in time, there was a chance that their differences could be resolved.

I made a mental note to ask Christine, and then immediately unmade it. This wasn't my remit so I should probably keep my nose out. This was respite; the girl was only going to be with us for a week. And, as alien as the situation was for me, maybe what I had here was one of those children in the fostering system who didn't really have many emotional problems at all – were in it simply as victims of circumstance.

Time would tell, but, again, I let the thought go, because a week wasn't enough time to 'tell' anything, was it? Well, except whether a makeover would be on the cards and (my brain started whirring now) whether one thing we could perhaps do was get Riley and Lauren over for some make-up related chit-chat. With Elise not in school we would have lots of hours to fill, after all.

Listen to yourself, I thought, as I took the proffered papers from Graham. Though a flash in Elise's eyes as he told me the full file would be with me as soon as possible made me also listen to that little voice that had dogged me from the start. I couldn't read it, but something meaningful had passed between them, I was sure of it.

Which, of course, begged another question. What?

Chapter 3

By the time I'd shown Elise around her bedroom and we'd come back downstairs, the file that Graham Baxter had left on my dining table was calling out to me. It wasn't the full file, of course, merely a care plan, a risk assessment and enough information about Elise's past so that we could do our best to keep her safe while she was with us. Still, the buff envelope that contained the paperwork was a great deal thicker than many I had seen recently, and I wouldn't be human if I had no interest in finding out more about her. So, I was happy enough when Elise asked me for the Wi-Fi password so that she could go up to her bedroom and get in touch with a few friends.

'I just need to let them all know I'm okay,' she said, as she sipped from the glass of squash I'd made for her. 'And that nothing horrible has happened to me. I ran out of data on the way over so haven't been on Insta for at least an hour.' She grinned at me. 'They'll all think I've been kidnapped or something!'

'There you go,' I said, passing her a little card with all the details on. I was rubbish with passwords so Tyler had printed some idiot cards out for me. At least, that's what he called them. They just contained the details of our Wi-Fi together with my and Mike's mobile numbers so that any foster kids could simply pop them into their phones. At one stage I'd suggested that I ought to pop the cards on bedside tables, just in case any children were too shy to ask, but Tyler had dissuaded me of that idea. 'If you'd done that when I moved in,' he'd pointed out, 'it would have just felt all wrong. Like I was in a B & B or a guesthouse. Not in a family.'

It was a good point. I smiled back at Elise. 'Go on, then,' I said, 'best get logged in without delay. We can't have your friends assuming you've been abducted by aliens, can we?'

Elise seemed thrilled with her card. 'Oh, how posh!' she trilled, turning it over between her fingers. 'I'm going to tell Jan to get some of these done so I can give them out to my friends when they visit. Oh, and Casey, thanks so much for letting me stay. It's a lovely room, and I'm sure we're going to have a lovely week together. And I meant it about the makeover. I could sort your brows out for you too.'

'I think you'd need a hedge-trimmer for that,' I joked, privately horrified by the prospect. Only once had I had my make-up professionally done, when I'd been maid of honour at my sister's wedding, and I could still recall the horror of seeing myself in the mirror – and of looking like a superannuated Barbie crossed with Coco the Clown. Never again. 'Hmm,' I said. 'We'll see.'

While Elise got herself settled in upstairs, I sat down at the dining table and reached for the paperwork, but before delving into it, I tried to pin down the feeling of unease that was seeping through me. First impressions are often highly inaccurate, and on the surface everything about this girl seemed to be great. Bubbly, quick to laugh, polite to a fault, and I'd noticed she kept eye contact as she was speaking, but … there was just something. I went through a quick mental checklist, trying to think of any other children she reminded me of. I often did this as it sometimes gave me an extra bit of insight if I recognised something in a child that I'd seen before, but not this time. I don't think I'd ever met any looked-after child that seemed to be brimming with this much confidence, and so happy and relaxed to be staying in the home of a complete stranger.

What I read, though, certainly seemed to endorse that well-known truth – that with kids what you see is not always what you get. This girl had been through the mill, and then some. I tried to imagine how it must feel to have almost every adult in your life claim that they couldn't or wouldn't care for you. How the constant moving around meant that friends were only there for short periods of time, sometimes only weeks.

The number of schools that Elise had attended showed that she had been the length of the county and everywhere in between. What really disturbed me, however, was a statement that one social worker had made, buried deep within the care plan. It said that during a conversation with Elise, the girl had disclosed, almost matter of factly, that she recalled once going to sleep in one friend's house and waking up in another. She admitted she had 'probably' been given drugs but couldn't be sure. I was bewildered to read on that, for some reason, this disclosure hadn't been followed up, nor had another disturbing claim the girl had made, that on quite a few occasions when she had been sleeping rough she had been sexually abused by strangers. This had been said to a teacher, who had, naturally, immediately alerted the authorities, but when an initial investigation had taken place, Elise had retracted what she had said. She had apparently then told the police that she had lied, and so was, it was concluded, simply 'an attention seeker'. More astounding, to my mind, was the footnote to it all – that no further action had been taken.

Why would that be? I couldn't help but ruminate on it. I knew that with girls as young as Elise was, the police would have to be alerted to such accusations, but I also knew from experience that if the girl refused to give names or addresses, and then retracted what she had said, there was nothing further they could do, apart from leave a card with a phone number and tell her to get back in touch if she needed to. I'd worked with some kids in the past who'd been prolific storytellers, with only a loose idea of what constituted the word 'truth'. Was this possibly the case with this girl?

So, though I could, and perhaps should, take Elise at face value, the next couple of days reinforced my initial suspicion that the happy, smiley Elise was a bit of a mask, because no one was this happy, not all of the time.

Yet, if there was more to this girl, it never once slipped. She was charming when she met Mike and charming over tea, and after retiring to her room to WhatsApp with friends and catch up with some telly, she came down to join me for breakfast the following morning, fully made-up and dressed – and, despite there being no school for her, at actual breakfast time! Something highly unusual in a teenager, in itself. She also offered to help and made sure she knew exactly how I took my coffee so that she could see to that while I boiled eggs and buttered toast.

She was talkative too, chatting away about this, that and the other – though I noticed she was careful to avoid anything that involved her own life, and instead talked about what was on the news, or on Instagram (where she followed various influencers, both in make-up and fashion), and even ventured an opinion on a then major political wrangle, leaving me open-mouthed – she knew more about the issue than I did!

Yes, this girl, on the surface, was every foster carer's dream child. Respectful and friendly, just on the right side of keeping herself to herself, and engaging fully when doing so was expected. And after the exact same thing happened on the second morning too, I began to suspect it was me who was the issue, that I'd become negative and cynical, looking for psychological damage where no damage existed. Perhaps this girl *was* what she seemed, a happy rarity.

Even so, when on the second day she asked me if she could go out and explore the area, I found it hard to put aside my instinctive anxiety about her being out and about solo – something I had no authority to stop her from doing. 'Why don't I take you out in the car?' I suggested. 'Show you round. Take you shopping. Would you like that?'

No, she wouldn't like that. She shook her head. 'I mean, yes, that would be nice, but you really don't need to worry. I'm a big girl,' she reassured me. 'And I'm fine on my own. And I promise if you ring me, I'll always pick up, and if you give me a time to be back, I'll never be late. Don't forget,' she added, 'I've spent a lot of time moving around, so I know how to look after myself.'

I had no doubt that she did, or at least that she thought she did, and because Christine had told me that Elise was fine out and about, I had really no choice but to allow her to go off alone. Which she did, for the rest of the day. Still, knowing how vulnerable she actually

I Just Want to be Loved

was – according to her file she was at risk of sexual exploitation, of course – I was on pins while she was away from the house – where had she gone? Who had she met? – and very grateful when she got back home on time.

The rest of the week continued in much the same way, with Elise never putting a foot out of place, and spending much of the daytimes out and about 'meeting mates'. And though she never elaborated on what she'd been up to, or who with, by the penultimate evening of the respite I remarked to Mike that I felt like a fraud getting paid to look after her.

'I've barely seen her,' I said, as I mashed potatoes for tea, 'and when I do, she's a delight to have around. You know, I'm starting to really envy Jan. I mean, when you think about some of the kids we've looked after.'

Mike laughed. Just home from playing football with Kieron and their five-a-side team, he was in a jovial mood. 'Love, trust me, you'd be bored out of your skull. Besides, don't speak too soon – there's still time for that makeover to happen. And, besides, don't forget – this sort of thing happens with respite. Some of ours have been angels when they've been away on respite.'

'Yes, I know *that*,' I said. 'But that's generally because they've felt insecure being away from us. This isn't like that. I know it isn't. She just seems so, well, *together*.' And I was just about to comment further when we both heard a sob. An anguished sob, loud and plaintive, coming from upstairs. Unmistakeably Elise.

We exchanged a glance. What had happened? I put down my masher, wiped my hands and hurried out into the hall. 'See?' whispered Mike, following me. 'What did I tell you?'

Chapter 4

Elise was halfway down the stairs when we arrived in the hallway, her face wet with tears and sooty trails of make-up. She was clutching one arm and looked completely distraught.

'Sweetheart,' I cried, 'what on earth is the matter?' I rushed to steady her as she stumbled down the last couple of stairs, then led her into the dining room and pulled a chair out for her to sit on.

Mike, who still had a jar of mint sauce in his hand, looked bewildered. 'Come on, sit,' I said. 'Is it a boy? Or an argument with a friend?'

I knew enough about teenagers to know that a simple online argument with a 'best friend' could cause unimaginable devastation in their minds. I was sure this must be the case, especially as she was never off her phone, but Elise was shaking her head and continuing to cry.

'Please let me stay here, Casey,' she blurted out, grabbing at my arms and pleading with her eyes. 'I promise I'll be as good as gold for you both, I swear I will, just please don't send me back to Jan's!'

That definitely threw me. Don't send me back to Jan's? Eh? Where the hell had this suddenly come from?

'Elise,' I said, gently, pulling another chair out and sitting down next to her, 'sweetie, you know you're only here for respite, for one week, don't you? And why on earth would you not want to go back to Jan's? She's lovely. And I thought you were happy there. What on earth has brought this on?'

'But you don't have any other kids in, Casey, do you?' Her wet-eyed gaze was fixed on mine. '*Please*. Let me stay, I can't go back there. I can't.'

She was tugging at the sleeve of her cardigan now. It was black, which was probably why I hadn't already noticed. It was sticking to her forearm and resisted as she pulled it. Then eventually it gave way, to reveal something that, in that instant, I guessed might be coming. A series of sticky, bloody cuts up her forearm. Cuts that were already clotting but which were definitely new – she'd been wearing a vest top that morning and I would have noticed. Was this what she'd been doing while I'd been getting on with dinner?

'Oh, Elise!' I said, reaching out to turn her arm so I could see the wounds better. 'What on earth have you done to yourself, love? *Why?*'

Mike put the jar of mint sauce down on the table with a clunk. 'I'll just go and put dinner on hold,' he announced. Code for 'your department, this one, so I'm going to leave you to it'. He never really knew what to say in situations like this, so I just nodded and turned back to the sobbing teenager.

'Well?' I asked, inspecting her wounds. 'You need to tell me what's brought all this on, love.'

Elise continued to sob as she drew her arm away and gently pulled her sleeve back down. 'I don't know,' she said. 'I just … just couldn't stop myself.'

'But why, love? What's happened? Why don't you want to go back to Jan's? I thought you were so settled and happy there.'

In answer she dissolved into sobs again. 'I'm not!'

'But why?'

'Because I'm *not*.'

'But, love, you need to tell me why. This doesn't make any sense.'

'But I can't. Because you're friends. And she'll get into trouble.'

Warming bells now began clanging in my head, and I knew I had to think before I spoke next. Clearly, Elise was worried about something, and that something – or someone – seemed to be Jan. Who I wasn't exactly friends with – not as personal friends, at any rate. We were just colleagues who got on and touched base when we met up at meetings. But Jan had always, to me, seemed perfectly lovely. She was also a very experienced foster carer, and extremely well respected. I couldn't imagine her doing anything even remotely untoward in a million years. Plus, I'd also read Elise's care plan. The bells rang out even louder.

'We're not "friends" friends, love,' I pointed out, using fingers to form quote marks, and trying to keep my tone light. 'At least, not like you think. We just know one another because we're both foster carers for the same team, but I cannot imagine how things could be so bad with you guys that you would have any reason to be worried about going back there. However,' I took her hand in mine and squeezed it, 'Elise, I'm here to listen, so please, lovely, tell me what's happened. What's caused you to do this?'

I then sat listening, stunned, as Elise poured it out to me. She claimed that Jan was 'weird', and that she would walk into Elise's bedroom, randomly and without knocking, claiming it was her house and she could do as she liked.

'The worst day was when she walked in on me while I was showering,' she went on. 'I've got a shower room off my bedroom and it doesn't have a lock, and she just … she just opened the door and walked in, and asked me if I had any dirty laundry!' She gripped my hand, tight. 'Please, Casey, phone Graham for me and tell him. I've made my mind up and I'm not going back there. I'm not. So, if you and Mike don't want me, he'll have to find me somewhere else. I mean it. I won't. I just *can't*.'

As horrified as I was feeling, because this certainly didn't sound like Jan at all, I tried to remain calm and expressionless. I stood up, telling Elise I was going to fetch my first-aid box. It would at least buy me a few seconds of time in which to think everything through.

'Roll that sleeve back up, sweetie,' I told her. 'I need to give your cuts a clean and take a good look at them, okay?'

She started doing as instructed as I left for the kitchen, where Mike was putting clingfilm over the dish of veg he'd strained. 'What gives?' he asked as I got the key down for the medicine cupboard.

'She's accusing Jan of being inappropriate, is what gives,' I whispered. To which his response was a sigh. That was his evening gone south.

I went straight back into the dining room and Elise was sitting where I'd left her, sleeve duly rolled up, the cuts crusting and congealing. I put the box on the table and found the pack of antiseptic wipes. 'So,' I said, 'as soon as I've dealt with these, I will telephone my link worker. Because it's her I need to speak with first, not Graham.'

'Thank you,' she whispered, wincing as the wipe touched the cuts. 'I'm so sorry. I just … ouch! Ow, that really, *really* stings.'

'I know,' I said, passing her a tissue. 'I'll try to be as gentle as I can, love.' And as I wiped, I realised that they were not deep cuts at all. I'd seen worse. Seen far worse. Seen life-threatening worse. These wounds were superficial – clearly not a serious attempt to harm herself. They had been, I judged, inflicted with the sole aim of getting my attention. And it had worked.

'Cutting is never the answer, you know,' I said, as I taped some dressings onto her forearm to keep the wounds clean. 'You can always tell me anything, love, and I honestly want to help you, but *please*, try not to do this again, Elise. You're so beautiful, and I know you wouldn't want to disfigure yourself, would you?'

A wan smile appeared through the tears. She shook her head. 'I know,' she said. 'And I'm sorry. I just didn't know what to do. It just kept building and building, and I thought I would burst. Please tell Mike I'm sorry too. I didn't mean to spoil your dinner.'

I closed the lid on the first-aid box, sensing a shift in the dynamic. A calmness about her. A plan executed. A job done. But *Jan*? There was little I could do but go along with it, however. 'Don't be silly,' I said, 'and I'll let you into a secret. Nothing spoils dinner for me – or Mike, for that matter. We like our food too much. And how about you? Are you up to eating something?'

She smiled again. But not too much. 'I *am* hungry, actually. I've felt so sick to my stomach, *so* sick I can't tell you. But now I've told you, I feel so, *so* much better.'

'Right then,' I said, decided. 'Let's get some food inside us, then, shall we? Then, once we're fed, I'll call Christine. How does that sound?'

'Thank you,' she said, dabbing at her face now with the tissue. 'Shall I finish laying the table?' she asked, reaching for the cutlery Mike had brought in earlier.

'Plan,' I agreed, little doubt in my mind now that she'd had one. Because as I sat and watched her chatting to Mike over tea a few minutes later, as if nothing had happened, I had a more than sneaking suspicion that I had been played by this teenager. I wasn't sure exactly why, and maybe I was wrong, but gone were the tears and the anguished looks, and back was the girl with the tinkling laugh and the hair flicks. There was definitely a lot more to this girl than met the eye. There always had been. And, by hook or by crook, she seemed determined to stay with us.

An hour later, Elise back in her room, and, if I wasn't mistaken, even laughing on the phone with friends, I explained everything to Christine Bolton, who sounded as shocked and dismayed as I was.

'That just doesn't sound right,' she agreed. Then she sighed. 'I mean, I'll obviously have to look into it. I'll have to let her social worker know too, of course, and then I'll have the grim task of telling Jan about the allegation, but I can tell you now, she's not going to take it too well.'

'Well, of course she won't,' I said. 'Neither would I in her position! To be honest, I'm astounded, and I just feel so sorry for her. I mean, odds are, given Elise's history, this is all a load of nonsense, or, at the very least, something innocent that's been misconstrued. But she'll still be put through it, because it will have to be taken seriously … oh, Christine, what a bloody mess.'

'A mess indeed,' Christine said, sighing again, this time heavily. 'And I'm sorry to have to lay something else on you too. If Jan's reluctant to have her back tomorrow – and I suspect she might well be – are you okay to hold on to Elise for a bit longer?'

It's a terrible thing to have a distraught child telling you about an awful experience they've had, but even more so when the accused is a fellow foster carer and you strongly doubt that the accusation is true. So even as I agreed to keep Elise for as long as necessary I was already feeling uneasy about the vulnerable position I was putting myself and Mike in. I'd already spoken to Mike about the possibility, and we were both prepared to be asked, of course, but what I couldn't fathom was the why of it all. If all of this proved to be untrue, and I didn't doubt it would be, why on earth would Elise do this when she clearly had everything she wanted at Jan's home?

Or, more accurately, what did she want so badly that she'd cut herself and tell lies to get it?

That was the question I didn't have an answer for.

Chapter 5

After my phone call to Christine, things happened very quickly – at least in terms of Jan being investigated and of us adjusting to the possibility of another complicated and challenging placement. Though when Christine called me again on the Tuesday morning to run everything by me, I decided I would be careful not to give Elise any false hopes, because I'd almost changed my mind when I found out what a shocking 48 hours Jan had endured.

Elise's social worker, Graham, had taken a telephone statement initially, asking the girl to be as detailed as possible about her allegations. But he didn't get very far; Elise became suddenly reluctant to speak and refused to reiterate what she'd said to me. That meant they didn't have an awful lot to go on, but, since she'd made the allegation and I'd reported it, they still had to approach Jan for her side of the story.

Jan, unsurprisingly, had been appalled and resolutely denied everything, but for her it sealed the deal in terms of continuing the placement – she wouldn't risk having Elise back, and I couldn't blame her, because such an allegation could harm, or even end, a foster carer's career. The toughest pill for any of us to swallow in the world of fostering was that even if an alleged incident was proven beyond doubt never to have happened, the whole thing got added into the annual review, and remained there for all to see, permanently on record.

So, we were left with Elise. At least for the short term. Whether she stayed with us long term was up to Mike and me, and though I had the usual internal tussle about whether it was wrong to refuse to keep her, her history of false allegations weighed heavily. How long before the same thing happened to us?

That said, those false allegations were also on *her* record, which, should we find ourselves in a similar position to Jan, would mean we at least had that evidence in our corner.

Needless to say, when she realised I'd just come off the phone to Christine, Elise was hovering anxiously, keen to hear her fate.

'They've agreed to let you stay with us for a bit longer,' I told her, 'at least until they decide the best course of action longer term, but nothing is set in stone yet. They have to run it by your social worker and management, but for now, you're staying with us.'

Elise almost knocked me flying as she threw herself at me. 'Oh, thank you so much, Casey!' she squealed, hugging me tightly. 'I promise you, I'll be as good as gold, you'll hardly know I'm here! And Graham will be absolutely fine about it – he really likes me, so don't worry about that. Oh, I'm so happy I don't have to go back to Jan's.'

I already knew the feeling was mutual as far as Jan was concerned, and I would soon find out exactly what she had to say about it, because shortly after the deal was sealed, and Elise had skipped off to meet her coterie of mates, Jan sent me a text, asking if I'd like to meet up in town the following Saturday, for a coffee and catch-up, when Mike would be at home to keep an eye on things.

'Blimey, Mum,' Tyler said, when Naomi dropped him home from their trip to York an hour later. 'You don't let the grass grow, do you? So, is she going to be long term now? She sounds like trouble.'

'Don't they all?' I laughed, deciding not to give him anything to worry about before I really knew the girl myself, though I made a mental note that he would need to be aware of her history at some point. 'But we always get there in the end, don't we?' I said, as I helped him drag his bags into the kitchen. 'Bloody hell, Ty!' I said. 'How long did you expect to be gone for? And no doubt all this lot needs washing?'

He grinned at me. 'Stop changing the subject, Mother dearest. You might always get there in the end, but it's the bits in between I worry about. Anyway, no rush with that stuff, I'm off back out to meet Denver for a catch-up.' He looked down at his well-travelled jeans and creased T-shirt. 'And he doesn't care if I stink, so I'll just go as I am.'

I shook my head as I watched him stride off straight back out the door again. Talk about ships that pass in the night! He'd been friends with Denver for years, so was obviously keen to see him, but I was still a bit miffed that, after being away with his girlfriend, he didn't want to stick around and tell *me* all about it. Or about any of it, in fact. He was in too much of a hurry to be gone. Then I gave myself a talking-to. He was an independent adult now. He didn't need to come home and confide everything to Mum. Plus, the fact that he wasn't was a good sign, in the scheme of things. It meant all was well, which was all I could ask for. Still, the loosening of those apron strings was always going to be hard, especially in conjunction with him having met a soulmate in Naomi. Again, very welcome, but a wrench for me even so.

So perhaps Elise had, in fact, come at the perfect time for me. And though she was older than Ty had been when he'd first come to us, their backgrounds had a lot, sadly, in common. Like Tyler, she'd been the collateral damage in an acrimonious adult relationship and had suffered the same kind of emotional neglect. She'd also been abandoned and had suffered at the hands of a less than loving stepmother, and though I still knew almost nothing of the details of her fractured childhood, the psychological landscape would almost certainly have been similar. In short, my suspicion was that this apparently 'together' teen had much in common with the eleven-year-old Tyler. And that knowledge, should we hang on to her, would all be useful.

The rest of the week passed in much the same way as the first had, with Elise, a sunny presence once again, behaving impeccably. And though I was cynical enough to know why she wasn't putting a foot wrong, day by day it made the decision-making easier.

I was still holding fire till I'd spoken to Jan, so when, on Saturday, while we settled down to lattes in my sister's coffee shop, I was pleased that she announced that she'd tell me all she could – in her words, 'the good, the bad and the ugly'.

And she definitely wasn't one to mince her words. 'I mean, honestly, Casey, I know we always complain that the child often turns out to be much more challenging than the care plan makes out, but in this case it was like they were describing a completely different girl.'

She was right about the inadequacy of care plans. It was as if they were very carefully worded to gloss over anything really bad, and concentrate more on the positive aspects of caring for such and such a child, and yes, I could understand the logic behind that, not just so a child wasn't tainted before they even got to you, but also because each child had a right to know what was on that plan, and, upon leaving care, could demand all of their paperwork. Nobody deserved to be carrying a file of information that would potentially be detrimental to the rest of their lives, and the carers also needed to know all the good bits.

However, I've always thought there should be some system designed, strictly for the eyes of potential carers, that could delve into all the less than rosy intricacies of each child, so they could better prepare for the challenges ahead. Instead, it seemed that the only way to get into all the nitty gritty on a child was to actually live it out, and then for foster carers to pass on information between themselves. Which was helpful, of course, but it wasn't the ideal system, as it was, by definition, after the fact.

I laughed. 'Well, you know you can spell it all out to me, Jan,' I said. 'We've had the same kids in the past so you know I can take it.'

Jan nodded. 'Oh, I know, but the thing with Elise is that it's so bloody difficult to put it into words. It's like she had her life and I had mine and, although we lived in the same house, we were a million miles away from each other. I never really felt as if I scratched the surface with her. I might as well have been running a B & B for all I felt I got to know the girl.'

'I feel the same,' I said. 'That she is constantly masking, and that the mask never slips.'

'I found it scary, if I'm honest with you,' Jan said. 'It was like living with an avatar. It's not the nicest way of putting it, but it was like absolutely everything I saw and heard from her was a lie. The sweet voice, the beguiling smiles, the hugs, the explanations, just everything. Every act or utterance seemed manufactured to suit her purpose – which was presumably to keep me sweet.'

'Superficial, then,' I offered, feeling much the same myself. Though, in reality, many kids were like this, especially at first, when moving in with a new family. Especially the really insecure ones, who'd been constantly moved around the system. And it wasn't so surprising. They obviously wanted to project the best version of themselves. But I got Jan's point. With Elise it was somehow different. The wall was so well constructed that there was no way to get in. 'So did anything specific happen – well, obviously, apart from the obvious – to make you think that?'

Jan drained her coffee and then signalled the waitress to order two more. 'No, nothing specific,' she said, 'but over time, I just came to realise how insincere she seemed. Almost as if she had curated a version of herself – like kids these days do on social media. I never felt I got beneath her skin. Except for one thing. The constant drama. If I had to give you just one word to describe her, that's what it would be. Drama. The girl seems to just exist for it, and if she doesn't have any going on, she'll create some.'

'She already did, remember,' I pointed out. 'Hence us two sitting here. D'you think that's what it was? That she just wanted to create some mischief because she was bored?'

'Very possibly. Perhaps she liked her room better at yours.'

I frowned, despite her quip. 'That's chilling. This is your professional reputation we're talking about. Not to mention potential criminal charges.'

'Hence my pulling out. And,' she added, frowning, 'throwing you under the bus instead. For which I'm sorry.'

Over the next hour, Jan poured her heart out, admitting that she had become weary of the placement even before the allegation, which, in many ways, she added, had been a blessing. 'You go into fostering hoping to make a difference, don't you? And in all the years I've been doing it, I've never felt so strongly that I wasn't. It really was just bed and board. No progress, and no connection. No sense that I was helping her move her life forward. Or that she even wanted me in it – well, except as a source of free food and Wi-Fi and money for clothes. And, sad to say, I didn't feel I got much support. All the time she wasn't causing headaches for anyone she barely registered, let alone be on the waiting list for any sort of intervention – even so much as trying to get her back into education. Anyway, give it a couple of weeks,' Jan concluded, 'and when Elise realises that she got her own way, she will actually tell you that she made it all up. It's her MO, always has been. The bloody times I've gone driving round to some person's house after she's told me this or that tale. A girl that's threatened to beat her up, a boy that's sexually molested her, a parent that's screamed at her in the park that they're going to slit her throat. Honestly, according to her, that girl's had more brushes with death than John McClane in bloody *Die Hard.*'

I couldn't help but burst out laughing at her analogy. 'Sorry, Jan,' I said, recovering myself. 'I know it's not funny. But you just put Bruce Willis in a vest into my head and I couldn't help it.'

Jan smiled. 'It was the only character I could think of,' she said. 'But it basically sums her up. And me, for that matter. The number of times I went charging around to all these places to follow up on Elise's claims, only to find they had absolutely no idea what I was going on about! So, I'd go back to Elise to ask what she was talking about, only for her to explain that this person or that person had annoyed her in some way, or even just *looked* like the type of person that might potentially attack her, so she'd made the whole thing up to 'teach them a lesson'! Can you *believe* that?'

'Wow!' I said, finally. 'So, she's definitely not a run-of-the-mill teenager then, and actually how *does* one include stuff like that on a care plan?'

'I know,' Jan said, sighing. 'I felt quite bad, to be honest. After the first few weeks I phoned Christine and ranted on for ages about how all this stuff had been missed out, but when I thought about it, like you say, how do you put things like that down on paper? And I suppose because she's moved around so much, there was never time to put any extra reports in alongside the usual paperwork. It's like when she was coming to you just for the week, I had to think about whether or not to

45

email you with some examples. In the end, I decided not, because I knew that for such a short time Elise would play nice and you wouldn't encounter any of this stuff.' She shrugged. 'But now, well, here we are.'

Here we were indeed. I had already told Christine Bolton that until I'd spoken at length with Jan, I wasn't prepared to say yes to a permanent placement for Elise, and even though I now had access to the huge file that went with the girl, there were a few things I wanted ironing out first. The most important of which I addressed with Elise the minute I got back into the house.

And once I told her where I'd been she was prepared. 'I bet she told you all kinds of lies about me,' she said. 'I wasn't lying, you know, not about her coming into my room. And maybe I got it wrong – maybe she didn't actually come *right* into the shower room, but I had *nothing on*. You don't *do* that. That's invasion of privacy. She had no business. And anyway –'

Unbelievable. I put a hand up to stop her saying more. 'The matter's closed now,' I told her. 'So, there's nothing to discuss. Jan's worried about you, that's all. About you getting into trouble. She –'

'God, what *now*?'

It was the first time I'd seen her on the defensive. And I didn't want to get involved in more drama from the past – nor Jan's parenting style, for that matter. So, I decided to be quite abrupt about veering things back on track.

'Look, Elise, I don't really want to talk about Jan, or any of the things that happened while you lived there, for that matter. I want to talk about the here and now, about the decision Mike and I have to make about fostering you full time. And there are two or three things that are stopping us from making that decision. That's what I wanted to talk to you about.'

Her expression changed completely, her features relaxing into a smile. 'Oh, that's great!' she said. 'Thank you *so* much. And whatever it is you want me to do, I'll do it, I promise.'

'Well, one thing is that I need to be sure that you will follow our most important house rule. The one every child here has to agree to. And that's to always answer your phone to me if you're out, and to always be back by the time we say. For our part, we will try to be fair about that, and negotiate a time with you, but the minute you let us down, Elise, we have to rethink it all, do you understand?'

'I swear to God I won't,' she said. 'I haven't so far, have I?'

'No,' I conceded, 'so far you haven't. But you need to keep that up, no exceptions.'

'I will, I will,' she promised.

'And I expect you to dress appropriately at all times when at home. No running around in your underwear, or skimpy night-things –'

I stopped. She was beginning to roll her eyes at me. 'Well, d'uh. Of *course*. I told you, when I was at Jan's –'

47

'This is nothing to do with Jan. It's a rule we have in place for every child who comes to stay here.' And is particularly pertinent in your case, I thought, but didn't add.

'Plus, one more house rule,' I said instead, 'which is particularly important. I need you to realise that I'm not running a guest house here. I'm not just your landlady, I'm your carer.' I stopped and thought for a moment before going on, wanting how I phrased this to be totally unambiguous. 'I know that sounds very formal, but, Elise, I don't want it to be. I'm here in place of your parents, as is Mike, of course, and I'd like you to treat us that way, okay? And as such, honesty, and talking about the important stuff, is what matters most to us. I want to get to know the real you, and equally you us, so anytime you feel like chatting, about anything, your past, or what's happening right now, or anything at all, basically, I'm here to listen, and so is Mike. Do you get that?'

Elise nodded vigorously at this. Perhaps a little bit too vigorously? 'Being honest with each other, basically,' she said. 'Yes, I get that. No problem.'

'Good. And the final thing is education. I've been told that you were excluded from your last school, and it's obviously up to you if you want to tell me why – remembering what we've just spoken about, of course – but I understand you've been refusing to go to any school since. I must be clear on this, Elise – going to school would be the deal breaker for us. We would need

48

you to get back into full-time education. And that's for your sake as much as ours. Even *more* than ours. You need to be in school, with other kids your own age, and to start catching up on your education. It will be a new start for you over here, and a new school, so there's no excuse not to.'

Her expression changed again, and it was difficult to read. What was she thinking? But then another smile appeared, a huge grin, in fact. 'And that's it?' she asked me. 'I come in when I'm told, wear a dressing gown, talk about the important stuff, agree to go back to school, and I'm here for good?'

I wavered a little then. Was I being too hasty? I still had no idea why she'd been excluded from her last school. Information I should surely demand *before* taking her on.

I could have kicked myself then for not asking Jan what she knew about Elise's exclusion from her last school, because I knew that, if she did know, she'd have told me.

What *was* clear, however, was that this was a troubled child who needed someone, even if she didn't acknowledge that herself. So where exactly *was* her head at? Despite my reservations, I was itching to get to the girl behind that sunny smile. The one who acted as if she hadn't a care in the world, but felt the need to make up stories all the time – including baseless and potentially damaging allegations about people. What did that say about her? That impulse and that lack of empathy worried me. But also, conversely, it made me actively want to get involved. It was connected to a past full of abandonment and rejection that, unexamined, might define her whole future. But it didn't have to be that way.

'That's it,' I said. 'So. Do we have a deal?'

'Deal,' she said, sticking a hand out for me to shake. And as I did so, I caught the smallest gleam of something like triumph in her eyes. She'd had an agenda, and she'd succeeded in fulfilling it.

Which was fine. Because she didn't know me yet, did she? So, she wasn't to know that I had one too.

Chapter 6

As I expected, Christine Bolton was happy that we decided to take on the placement and she agreed that school was a necessary part of the deal, so the next week meant a flurry of paperwork being sent back and forth – new agreements and placement plans, along with the usual risk assessment, and then another visit from Graham, Elise's social worker.

'How do I look?' Elise asked him once she joined us in the dining room. He lowered his eyes and appeared to be embarrassed. 'Very nice,' he said. 'But aren't you a bit cold in just that?'

I silently agreed. While we'd been going through some of the paperwork, Elise had got herself changed from what she'd been wearing earlier in the day. Before I'd told her that Graham was calling, she'd been wearing some lovely red tracksuit bottoms with white stripes down the sides, along with a new white T-shirt (her favourite kind, it seemed) that I'd bought her the day before. Now, she had on a pair of cut-off denim shorts that left very little to the imagination, and a skimpy cropped top, plus her sporty trainers had been replaced with a pair of high-heeled wedges. She also now had on full make-up and false eyelashes and her hair was being held off her face by her designer sunglasses.

'Elise!' I said, 'I know it's May, but it's hardly warm enough for those, love, and honestly, you'll break your neck in those shoes!'

Elise giggled coquettishly. 'Oh, Casey,' she said, 'you sound like my flipping nan! All my friends dress like this – it's what you call "fashion".' She obligingly put the word in finger quote marks for me.

It was, I noted, the first time she'd mentioned her nan, and I made a mental note to ask Christine what the state of play was regarding her operation and the possibility of re-establishing regular contact. There was no time like the present when it came to repairing family relations, after all.

Graham, meanwhile, was in the middle of a timely coughing attack. 'Come on, then, Elise,' he said, gesturing towards an empty dining chair once he'd recovered, 'you look like you have things to do, places to be, and I certainly have, so let's get down to business.'

Elise pulled a face as she sat with us, and groaned at him theatrically. 'This is about school, isn't it?' He nodded, and she raised her hands, in dramatic submission. 'I know, I know, it's part of the deal and I promised.

And I will definitely go,' she said, glancing at me. 'It's just it's been so long, and I'm nervous as hell. I mean, I won't know anyone, will I?'

'Well, no,' I said, 'you won't at first, but, Elise, from all I know about you, it won't take you two minutes before you start making new friends.' I looked at Graham hopefully then. 'So, you've found a school already? Is it local?'

Graham nodded a second time, and I sent a silent vote of thanks up to the heavens. School places for looked-after children had to be found, but, particularly for kids with a less-then-rosy history of attendance, definitely did not grow on trees. 'I think so,' he confirmed. 'At least, it's looking very promising. They've agreed to a meeting in the next week or two – it might have to wait till after half-term – with the head, head of year, myself, you and Elise. And if that goes well, it seems that as soon as she has a uniform, Elise can start. And yes, it's local. In fact, I think it's the one you used to work at, Casey.'

Elise gaped at me. 'Are you a *teacher*?'

I wasn't sure whether to feel piqued that she apparently found this possibility so unlikely. 'Kind of,' I said. 'I used to run the behaviour unit there.'

'What's a behaviour unit?'

The sort of place where I suspect you might have spent time, I thought. 'A place for all the children who struggle in mainstream classes,' I explained. 'The bullied, and sometimes the bullies as well. Kids with problems at home. Kids with special educational needs. All sorts, like the liquorice – children who have problems learning in the conventional sense.'

Though the potential wait was disappointing, I was thrilled that Graham had convinced them to see us, especially as Elise was new to the area and had been excluded permanently from her last school; pulling off that sort of trick usually took a lot more than a phone call from a social worker. Best of all, it was within walking distance of home, so it was perfect. No traipsing across town every day.

'It's a great school,' I told Elise now. 'You'll love it.'

Elise didn't look so enthusiastic, however, and she was quick to point out why.

'I'm not being funny or anything, Casey,' she said, 'but that makes it ten times worse! Can you imagine the stick I'm going to face when all the other kids find out my foster mother used to work there?'

'It was years ago,' I said, 'so you don't have to worry about that. I bet there's no one left there who even remembers me. So don't stress. You'll be absolutely fine there.'

'Anyway,' Graham said, 'like I said, it's going to be at least a week before we even have the meeting, but fingers crossed it all goes well. Then I'm sure you'll fit in quickly and make some friends.'

'Some *more* friends,' Elise pointed out. 'I do *have* a few, you know, Graham.'

To which I was sure he was about to reply, 'Don't I know it?' But he held his tongue and wrapped the meeting up instead.

Graham's visit was a statutory one. Even when a social worker escorts a child to a new placement, by law they have to visit within seven days to check that everything is working out. A paper-ticking exercise that I was well used to but never really had any high expectations over. This time, however, it had brought good news, so I was on quite a high as I went to the door to wave Graham off.

'Thanks so much for working so quickly to get her back into school,' I said. 'I'm sure she must be bored senseless already, stuck in here or her room with nothing to do.'

'Oh, I wouldn't worry too much about that,' he replied, chuckling. 'Our girl in there never gets bored, rest assured. In fact, unless I'm very much mistaken, she will already have a vast network of brand new online friends, just waiting to meet her.'

Graham gave me a jokey wink and laughed as he left. 'Don't look so alarmed, Casey,' he said. 'You and Mike are more than capable of dealing with the shenanigans of teenage girls like Elise. It'll all be fine, I'm sure. Keep the faith.'

I thought, but didn't say, that the only thing I had faith in when it came to fostering was the high probability that shenanigans, as he'd put it, were likely to happen. But with school now on the horizon, I felt ready for it.

I also imagined Graham was right about Elise's huge number of virtual friends – being out of school, she had the time to live a parallel life online, and so it seemed she had, as I was to find out a couple of days later, when Riley phoned with a pretty everyday request. She wanted to know if I was on any local marketplace groups, and if so, if I could look out for any baby toys. Kieron and Lauren's baby Carter was into everything now, and as Riley helped them out once a week with babyminding she wanted to lay hands on some inexpensive toys to keep at home for him, having already offloaded her own stash to a friend.

'Wooden blocks, stuff he can bash and sort, make towers from – you know the sort of thing,' she said. 'So, if you see any advertised can you grab them for me?'

Which was why I was trawling the local selling pages that afternoon, and why I noticed there was a local girl selling baby toys. I was just about to click on her pictures to get a better look, when I noticed the thread of comments on her latest post. At first I thought I'd read it wrong, but no, it was definitely Elise commenting. And our Elise – it was clear from her profile photo. So, I started reading. She'd started out asking about a baby tracksuit the girl had for sale, and asking what size it was, then commenting that it was a shame, but that it was too small. I was obviously puzzled – she'd yet to meet any of the family apart from Tyler, so who was she potentially buying baby clothes for? But reading on it seemed that was just a conversation starter; a few posts on she admitted that she was new to the area and was keen to try and make some new friends. She said she was lonely and stuck indoors all day – not even remotely accurate! – and would love to meet up if the girl was free one day. To which the girl said of course – that she'd love to meet for coffee and could even maybe introduce her to some of her friends.

I felt taken aback. Was this really what she was doing up in her bedroom? I felt quite sorry for her, too – I didn't know a lot about the various ways teenagers connected these days, but to me it seemed a desperate move to join a local selling site simply to find people to chat to. I also felt a kind of respect, though. It was hard when you were lonely to reach out to complete strangers, and because of that veneer of breezy confidence it was a side of her I'd never seen before. A definite chip in the veneer.

So, I resolved that I should help her, if I could. She'd been out most of the morning – to meet the girl for that coffee? – but when she came home for lunch I decided I'd mention it.

'I hope you don't think I was stalking you or anything, love,' I said as I passed a bowl of salad across the table, 'but I was online on a local selling site, looking at toys for my grandson, and guess whose face popped up on there? Yours! And I noticed you were chatting to a girl on there. Do you know her from somewhere else?'

Elise's smile didn't falter. 'Oh God, no!' she said. 'That girl's got a kid, and she's single! But she probably knows people in the area. And she seemed the sort who'd talk to pretty much anyone, so I thought if I'm going to be going to school here, I'd best use her to get to know some locals. Find out who's good, who's bad, who's popular and stuff.' She then grinned as she clocked my by now bemused expression. 'It's *fine*, Casey, honest. I know what I'm doing. It really is the best way to get to meet new friends. I do it all the time.'

'You do? What, join selling sites and start chatting to random people wherever you live?'

She nodded, as she doled herself out some salad. 'Well, yeah, but not just the selling sites. Others too. I build up my friends list from the ones who chat back, or the good-looking boys, and then usually we start messaging, and *voila*!' She beamed at me. 'New friends.'

As Elise started to list the names of the sites she had joined locally, I was thinking that the idea was either quite ludicrous or very clever, but then she named one that I'd never heard of – one that started the alarm bells ringing overtime.

'Wait, what?' I asked. 'Did you say "thieves and thugs"? That's a local site round here, is it? And you've joined it?'

Again Elise laughed, and this time it was apparently at my naivety. 'Well, duh!' she said. 'I'm not going to have any fun just meeting the local goody two-shoes, am I? Don't worry, Casey, I know you're old-fashioned, but we young people like to know right from the start who's good and who's bad, like I said. No point doing it the old way where you think you're getting to know someone and then later find out they're like a drug dealer or something. Best to cut all that waiting out and know straight away. People do that stuff nowadays. Everyone puts it out there for the world to see.'

I closed my by-now open mouth. I was truly shocked, both at the knowledge that we had such a site locally, and also at the matter-of-fact way Elise had just described what she clearly perceived to be a normal way of making friends. I wondered if my Riley or Kieron were aware of any of this, or were they in fact 'too old-fashioned' as well. I would ask Tyler. He was closer to Elise in age. So, if anyone could tell me, it would be him.

'Well, maybe they do,' I conceded as I watched Elise eating her salad as though she hadn't just dropped an enormous bombshell, 'but still, I don't think it's an entirely safe way of meeting people. You read all the time about old men pretending to be young girls in order to deceive them and meet up with them.'

'That's a *whole* other type of chat site, Casey,' Elise said, her mouth twitching in amusement. 'Why on earth would they use fake profiles on a site selling clothes and toys?'

I felt a bit silly then, because she was probably right, but it had unnerved me a bit, so later, when Tyler came home from work, I tackled him about it straight away.

'I suppose some people get chatting for the first time on sites like that,' he acknowledged, 'but no, I can't think of anyone who would purposely join a selling site just to make friends, and yes, I'd definitely try to keep her off that *thieves and thugs* group. She's right, it's full of all the local idiots and druggies, thinking they're all big and hard because they have police records. Thing is, it proves how stupid they are because I've heard the site is monitored by the cops, which they love because it means they have them all rounded up in one place. Nobody I know would join that site.'

But Elise had, and now I had that to worry about. I knew I couldn't stop her if that was what she was doing but, mindful of the sort of thing Jan had had to deal with, I made another mental note to add another 'deal breaker' to our conditions of habitation. Do *not*, under any circumstances, give out our address to any of these new so-called friends.

Then I went to get my laptop. I was also in need of a bit of education.

Chapter 7

The next few days seemed to fly by, and my anxieties about Elise, and the double life she seemed to lead, were starting to really build up now. At home, she was this well-spoken, smiley, delightful young lady who seemed to only want to please, yet out on the streets – where she went to seek out or meet these new 'friends' – I had a feeling that she was a completely different personality. She'd invariably come home with bad things to say about one person or another and Jan's warnings couldn't help but come back to me. Telling tales really did seem to be a compulsion with this girl; I was beginning to realise that with her dim view of the world she'd find something to offend her in an empty room.

As I was learning, she was also the master of subtle manipulation. 'God, what is *wrong* with me?' she asked one day as she appeared in the back doorway after being out for the afternoon. I was in the garden, on my knees, pulling weeds from my beleaguered flowerbeds. We'd had a long dry spell, and while the bedding plants I'd so painstakingly put in kept wilting, the weeds had had a field day, running rampant along the borders. Re-wilding, I think they call it these days.

Since the way Elise had spoken seemed rhetorical, and therefore didn't strictly require an answer, I didn't offer one, not immediately. 'In what way?' I asked instead. 'Because that's a fairly big question.'

Kicking off her sandals, Elise marched barefoot across the grass. I looked up at her, having to squint against the sun's late-afternoon glare.

She flumped down on the grass, her tanned colt-like legs folding up beneath her. 'Actually, no,' she said. 'What's wrong with *boys* is the question. I mean, I can't help the way I look, can I? And I shouldn't have to anyway, because that's victim-blaming, and that's wrong. It's not girls who need to worry about what they wear and what they do. It's *boys*. They just think they can take whatever they fancy, and –'

'Love, slow down,' I said, sitting back on my heels so I could study her. She was clearly agitated, sighing to herself and plucking up little clumps of grass. 'What exactly's happened? Who's upset you?' A heavier sigh. And a silence. And I couldn't help but think *here we go* … 'A boy, I presume?'

Elise nodded. 'Luke.'

'Luke?' I was finding it hard to keep track of all the new names she bombarded me with daily.

'Luke Armitage,' she clarified, leaving me not at all the wiser.

'And what's this Luke done?'

Another lengthy silence, then, abruptly, she stood up again. 'I don't want to talk about it. I just need a shower. Is it okay if I have a shower?' And, if I wasn't mistaken, she shivered. No. Correction. It was definitely more of a shudder. Then she hovered there, as if waiting for me to react.

'Of course, love,' I said, clambering up now as well. I was about to ask her if she wanted to tell me something else but then it suddenly hit me – was she baiting me? She shuddered again then, and in such a way that it confirmed my suspicion that she was waiting to see if she could coax me into whatever drama she was keen to expand on. And then and there I decided to ignore the body language and instead take her at her word. She said she didn't want to talk about it, so I wasn't going to press it. 'Go ahead,' I said instead. 'There's plenty of hot water.'

And the way she turned around so abruptly seemed to confirm it. I watched her go back across the garden, feeling vindicated but also torn. Should I have tried to coax something more out of her? Should I try to do so later? I wasn't sure. Perhaps I should simply wait and see if she brought it up gain. I felt sure that this was just the kind of drama Jan had told me about, but on the other hand, despite how Elise came across, she was fourteen and vulnerable, and as such I really ought to try to get to the bottom of things. Damned if you do and damned if you don't! I made a mental note that if she said nothing further that night, to bring the subject up again after she'd had the chance to sleep on it. As it happened, it was the very next morning. And not at all in the way I expected.

Elise had just come downstairs for breakfast, and was clearly already on FaceTime, chatting to a teenage boy as she came into the kitchen and, as she sat down, propping her phone against her glass of orange juice. I had no idea who the boy was that was smiling uncomfortably at me through the screen.

'Say hi to Casey!' Elise trilled as I passed behind her to get to the fridge. 'She's my carer and she's super-cool!'

'Hi,' I said to the boy, quickly moving out of shot and getting the milk out to put in the coffee I'd just made.

'Casey's *mad* about coffee,' Elise told the boy chattily. 'Proper addicted. Aren't you?' she added, smiling across at me.

'You could say that,' I agreed, not wishing to get embroiled in their chat. 'Anyway, I'll leave you guys to it. Don't want to gatecrash your conversation.'

'Oh, it's *fine*,' Elise told me as I put the milk back in the fridge. 'Anyway, so you've done it then? Told the slag where to go?'

This was turning into the sort of conversation I both did and didn't want to listen to. I was also struck by the way Elise didn't seem to care whether I heard it. Though the boy obviously did because his answer to this was mumbled and swiftly followed by him saying that he really had to go as his mum was apparently shouting for him.

'Okay,' Elise said. 'So, I'll meet you outside college on your lunch break, then, yes?'

'I'll ring you and let you know,' came the answer, immediately. 'I don't know if I'm going in today.'

'Seriously? But I thought you said you were. Anyway, I –'

'I'll call you. I have to go.'

The call ended abruptly. 'Well, *fine*,' Elise said to his now frozen image. She was clearly unimpressed at being so summarily dismissed.

I leant against the worktop and sipped my coffee. 'So. Who was that, then?'

'Just Luke,' she said.

Luke? I nearly spat my coffee out. 'Luke as in the boy you were complaining to me about yesterday?'

Elise flapped a hand dismissively. 'Oh, that was just a little argument. He started a relationship with me before he'd actually finished with his ex, and oh my God, you should see her – she's *gross*! He's finished with her for good now though because he wants me, but no doubt she'll be trying to stir up some shit for me – and when *she's* the one who cheated on him first – with Nathan Collins. Oh my God, she's *such* a slag, she really is.'

65

As usual when listening to one of Elise's commentaries, my head was now spinning. I had no clue who was who, or what had happened, much less when or where, but I had picked up on one thing. A quite important thing, too. At least in my book.

'Luke's at college then, is he? How old is he, Elise?'

'Seventeen? Maybe eighteen. I'm not exactly sure.'

'A little old for you, don't you think, love?' I gently suggested.

She slipped her phone into her bag, shaking her head as she did so. 'No one in their right mind goes out with boys their own age – they're like *babies*.'

Yes, I thought, as opposed to ones who are intent on making them, which, given her comments the previous evening, felt pertinent.

This was the central frustration when fostering teenagers. Where a parent held some sway over what their teenagers got up to and who with (and quite right too), as foster carers we had no such authority. We couldn't forbid them from going somewhere, we couldn't ground them and we definitely couldn't take their phones, even if we knew they were accessing things they shouldn't be. It was parenting with both hands tied behind your back. Yes, we could ask them where they were going, and perhaps for a friend's number, if they were going to their house, say, but if they were lying to us there was frustratingly little we could do. What they shared with us was up to them and the only 'weapon' in our armoury was to keep the communication channels open and hope some of our advice to them sunk in.

Since Elise was so candid I decided to be as forthright as she was. 'Love, last night you made out to me that you'd had to fight off unwanted sexual advances from this lad, and that you wanted nothing more than to get a shower and forget him.'

Elise stared at me, her lips quivering as though she might cry. 'Well, I know I didn't say those *actual* words, Casey, and if that's what you got, then I'm sorry. We'd just had an argument, that was all, and I was upset. But I *do* love him.'

I hid my reaction of course, but seriously – she *loved* him? As far as I could tell, she'd known him all of two bloody minutes.

'Well, just be careful, love,' I said, topping up her orange juice. 'Older boys, while they seem mature, can have expectations that might be scary to a younger girl, so just make sure you do know what you're doing. And remember' – in for a penny, I thought: I might as well be frank with her – 'if he has sex with you – a fourteen-year-old – he is breaking the law.' I paused to let that sink in. 'So. *Does* Luke know how old you are?'

I saw a flicker of irritation in her eyes. Which made sense. The very point of all those hours spent primping and polishing were about being able to pass herself off as older than her years. The very last thing Elise wanted – at least, that was my hunch – was for anyone to find out her real age. Plus, she wasn't in school. So how

67

could her 'friends' know? I resolved then and there to press harder for that school meeting. And soon. Because that was where a fourteen-year-old needed to be. Not out on the streets, playing grown-ups.

And what she said next couldn't have pressed the point more firmly home. Nor make it any clearer to me just how young and naive she really was. 'You know I've had sex, right?' she asked, looking straight at me, as if hoping to shock me. 'I'm not some scared little kid who doesn't know what's what. I've *lived* life. I know how to look after myself.'

Oh, how the world has changed, I thought. Since when did it become remotely acceptable for a four-teen-year-old girl to casually drop into conversation with an adult that she was sexually active? I thought back to when Riley had been that age and knew that she would have been mortified at such a conversation. She used to make sick sounds if we were ever watching a movie and a couple were kissing on the TV. But the world had changed. There was no doubt about that. With the whole internet at their disposal via the phones in their pockets, adolescents didn't just have the keys to the information kingdom – they could see things they shouldn't, have access to terrible misinfor-mation and, worst of all, have it help shape their ideas of what was normal; and all while their brains were still developing.

In short, we adults had to get used to a world where the goalposts were constantly moving. So many lines that never used to be crossed were now dust, and though boundaries still had to be set, and we would set them, we had to be realistic about our expectations.

Shocked, though? She had addressed the wrong person. 'Your sex life is none of my business,' I told her. 'Your safety, however, very much is. And will remain so for as long as you live with us, obviously, so if there's ever anything that worries you, or things you need to talk about, I'm always happy to listen. In the meantime, whatever else you do, please, *please* be safe.'

To which Elise smiled and pointed to a small scar in her upper arm.

'Thanks,' she said, smiling, 'but it's fine. I've got an implant. So, you don't need to worry about me getting pregnant or anything.'

That wasn't what I meant about keeping safe, but I supposed it was something, though I was surprised no one had told me she had an implant. I figured it was probably somewhere on her file and I must have missed it. I would clearly have to sit down and go through it all again.

Once she'd gone off to wherever she was going to – to meet Luke or otherwise – a cloud of weariness began to settle over me. I was beginning to see what Jan had meant about not being able to make a difference. What exactly *could* I do to make a difference in this strange young girl's life?

I could hope, I supposed. Hope that school, once she got a place, made a difference. Hope that she stuck at it and even worked at it. Hope that an educational worker would be allocated to her pronto and that her PEP (Personal Education Plan) would be updated and passed on. Hope relations with her grandmother – and even perhaps her parents – could be repaired. Hope, just like everyone, for the best.

I spent the rest of the day doing chores and writing up notes on my daily sheets, making sure I recorded everything that had been said that morning. I almost sent the sheets off in the afternoon, without waiting for Elise to get back, but something made me click on 'save' rather than 'send', and that evening, I was glad that they were still on my computer, because it turned out that there was a lot more writing left to do.

It was about 9 p.m. when the commotion started. Tyler hadn't been feeling very well and had taken himself off to bed not long after dinner, and Elise, as she always did, had gone to her own room at 8 p.m. Mike was watching a programme about ice road truckers and I was pottering around in the kitchen, making his and Ty's packed lunches for the next day, when I was sure I heard raised voices coming from upstairs.

Mike must have heard it too because I heard the volume of the TV go down, then he appeared in the kitchen, nodding back towards upstairs.

'Is it Elise arguing with someone again?' I asked, sighing wearily. 'I'm going to have to speak to her about that and respecting everyone else in the household. It's not on.'

Mike cocked his head slightly. 'That's Tyler talking. Listen!'

We both went into the hall, to hear the argument beginning to escalate.

'You're old enough and intelligent enough to know better!' Tyler shouted, 'and it's not the first time you've done it, either. You're out of order, and you know it.'

'What are you, *gay* or something?' Elise shouted back as Mike and I ascended the stairs. 'I don't know what your problem is. It was an *accident*, alright?'

I was already halfway up the stairs when I shouted, 'What the hell is going on?' It wasn't at all like Tyler to have a go at anyone, let alone a child who was living with us, so I knew it must be something.

Elise had already gone back into her room – Ty was standing in the doorway of his – but now she re-emerged back onto the landing wrapped in a towel. I looked at Tyler and spread my arms. 'What happened?'

Elise was grinning now, as though waiting to hear what Tyler had to say, and was enjoying how uncomfortable he looked.

'She –' he began, raising a finger. But she immediately talked over him.

'*I'll* tell you what happened, Casey,' she said. 'Your son seems to think I'm a *mind reader* is what happened, and that I know every time he decides to leave his room.'

I looked back to Tyler, confused.

'That's not how she was covered up two minutes ago,' he said, clearly very angry. 'She was only in her under-wear, and she waited until I was coming out of the bathroom before she walked across the landing. She *waited* for me to come out. It's not on, Mum,' he finished. 'You need to have a word.'

Now *I* was angry. I might not know the exact circum-stances, but what I did know was that Elise was well aware of the dress code in a fostering household, because I could not have been clearer in explaining that to her. She was not supposed to wander around in her underwear outside of her bedroom. At *any* time. It was as simple as that. Plus, it was right there, in writing, on our very short house rules list, along with always answering the phone to me and not being in late: *dress appropriately at all times around the home and use a dressing gown over nightwear.*

A horrible thought slammed into my head. That I was a fool. With my insistence on our house rules, had I been the one to give her the idea? Judging by her expression, it was possible. 'And I most certainly will,' I told Tyler, while glaring at Elise. 'In your bedroom,' I added to her, 'after you've put something on.'

'Okay,' she said, flouncing back in, while Tyler rolled his eyes at me, before stomping off back into his own room.

'I'll leave you to it then,' Mike said, turning back and down the stairs again, very sensibly doing just that.

'He's right, Elise,' I said as I followed her into her bedroom. 'And don't pretend you don't know better, because you do.' She opened her mouth to speak, and I immediately held my hand up to stop her. 'And before you tell me you didn't know he was in the bathroom, that's entirely beside the point. You don't walk along the landing in just your underwear anyway. You have a dressing gown, or you could have pulled some trackies on, or anything. Love, when you live in a house with others, you have to respect their privacy. Just as they respect *your* privacy. Do you understand?'

'Fine!' Elise said, still defiant. 'But it's not like he hasn't seen it before, is it? He has a girlfriend, doesn't he? I just don't know what the fuss is about. It was an accident and it's only like wearing a flipping bikini!'

'I'm not arguing with you about it,' I said. 'You know the house rules, and I don't expect it to happen again, okay?'

Another 'Fine!' and a (yes, very much fourteen-year-old) face pulled, but at least I'd said my piece. I went to check on Tyler before going back downstairs.

He looked wretched. 'I'm sorry about that, Mum,' he said, 'but I swear, honest to God, she waits for me, I know she does. This is the third time she's done it. No *way* is it accidental.'

'I know, sweetie,' I said, 'and I'm sorry. I've been very clear with her about the rules though, so hopefully she'll be embarrassed enough not to do it again now.

And I'll record it in my notes too, so it's written down. Okay?'

It was not okay. 'Mum, that girl is trouble,' Tyler said. 'And with her history of making false allegations, I'm like a flipping sitting duck! She could say anything about me and how could I defend myself? It would be my word against hers. And you know how it works. Doesn't matter if it's rubbish, it would still have to be investigated.'

'I know, love,' I said, 'but, like I said, I'll record this. The more she cries wolf, then the less her word counts. And if need be,' I added, trying to think on my feet, 'we'll relocate her to the conservatory, like Jenna and her little ones. In fact, perhaps I'll tell her that if she's caught wandering around in her underwear again that's exactly what *will* happen.'

Which mollified Tyler, at least a little. 'Though I'd be happier if you moved her downstairs *now*,' was his opinion, and though I told him I was sure she would desist now I'd spoken to her, as I went back downstairs I wasn't convinced. This, as Jan had told me, was her MO, after all. Perhaps a greater threat was needed; that if she did it again, we would ask that she be moved from us altogether. However much I might want to do my bit for this child, I had my own child to think about, and that mattered more.

Mike agreed. 'Ty's right, love,' he said. 'We have to protect him – *and* us – against anything she might say. It's bloody scary!'

I agreed. And I needed to nip it in the bud.

Decided, I retraced my steps back up the staircase, knocked on Elise's door and, when she answered, went in there.

She was lying on her bed, on her back, legs crossed at the ankle, and her 'What?' still held a definite note of defiance, confirming my belief that I was right to come back up. And right too, to make my position crystal clear.

'I just wanted to have another word, love,' I said, as she wriggled up to a sitting position. 'About actions and consequences, just so we both know where we stand.' And even as I said it I knew it made sense to go further than to just threaten to relocate her to another part of the house. 'You must be appropriately dressed any time you are not in your bedroom,' I continued. 'And –'

'I know,' she interrupted. 'You already told me. And I promised I would be, didn't I?'

I nodded. 'Yes, you did, love, but I don't want you to be in any doubt. If any of us catch you in your under-wear on the landing again – or in any other similarly inappropriate place in the house, for that matter – I will call Graham and tell him you can no longer stay here. No ifs. No buts. No excuses. Is that clear?'

She exhaled heavily and for a moment I expected a curt rejoinder. None came, however. Just a small, submissive nod, her demeanour such that I wondered if I'd been a bit too harsh.

'Good,' I said. 'Sleep tight, love.' And then I left her.

And as I headed down the stairs I was glad I'd been back up. Elise's records had taught me lots, and one of the main things I'd learned was that this wasn't a girl to whom you gave the benefit of the doubt.

Which felt harsh as well, but the line needed drawing. If we were going to help her she needed to know it had been and that it wouldn't be drawn again.

Chapter 8

Regardless of my worries about unfounded allegations, life had to go on, and Elise had to be looked after. We had made a commitment to foster her now, and that could mean for a long time – *should* mean for a long time, in fact. After deciding as a family that we all had to simply be on our guard, and to ensure we weren't ever put into a situation that could be misconstrued, we had to get on with it and learn to adapt to this newcomer to our family. As I often told my mum and dad, fostering wasn't a pick and mix – a child in need was a child in need. Many times my mum would purse her lips, fold her arms and shake her head, saying, 'Oh, Casey, you don't half pick them, love! Why can't you ever just get a good kid?' And each time, I would sigh and try to explain about how kids weren't 'bad', they just came from bad situations, and that beneath their behaviour was a frightened and traumatised child, one just yearning to be nurtured and loved.

And, for all that she strove so hard to pass herself off as an adult, that was exactly what Elise so surely was.

There was good news, however, the following Monday, when Graham called to let me know he'd arranged a school meeting for that Friday, with a view to Elise starting in school the following week. But that still left a full week with her at large and at liberty, and a great deal could happen in a week. So, I found myself looking into my mirror every morning and repeating a mantra I hadn't used for years: *You can do this, Casey. Today will be a good day.* Then I would go downstairs and start my routine of making breakfast while cleaning up, then I'd call Elise down to join me, then wait for her to announce her plans for the day. Because there were always plans. Some I dreaded, and some made me sigh with relief, such as the Tuesday when it was raining, and she told me she was spending the day at home, cleaning her room and watching movies. Some parents would be horrified that I preferred that option for a fit and healthy teenager, but the alternative, like the following morning, set my every nerve jangling.

'So yeah, I'm meeting Ryan at half eleven,' Elise informed me, while slicing the top from her boiled egg. (One thing I didn't have to worry about. She ate like a horse.) 'Oh, Casey, you'd like him, he wears full Adidas from top to toe!'

'Not Luke, then?' I asked her.

Elise spluttered theatrically. 'OMG, Casey! You almost made me choke on my toast then! He's *such* a loser. No, I dumped him. I'm seeing Ryan now. He doesn't go to college, so he doesn't get tempted by all the little tarts doing hair and beauty, but, oh, he's *so* gorgeous. I'm surprised he's single, to be honest.'

My heart sank somewhere deep in my chest. 'But he goes to school? Please tell me this one is closer to your own age.'

Elise shook her head and gave me what some might interpret as a pitying look. It meant: *You just don't get it, do you?* Then she spelled it out to me, too. 'I told you,' she said patiently, 'I don't *go* for boys my own age. I much prefer older lads. They know what they want, and they don't play games for weeks like silly schoolboys do. If they like you, they just ask you out and that's that, no messing around.'

'So how old is this Ryan boy?'

'He's not a boy.' She grinned at me. 'He's eighteen.'

I tried to think of something to say that sounded non-judgemental, but I was struggling. 'Sweetie, I know what you're saying, but I do think eighteen is too old for you. And fourteen, to my mind, is too young for *him*. Yes, I know you're very mature for your age, but you *are* still only fourteen, and four years is a huge gap right now. I mean, yes, down the road, when you're maybe eighteen yourself, that four-year gap will mean very little, but right now, it's a significant difference.'

But, much as I'd anticipated, my words fell on deaf ears. Elise just thought I was old-fashioned and didn't understand the way the world worked in 'this day and age'. In fact, she went as far as to say that I really ought to consider always fostering teenagers, as opposed to little kids, because then I might understand them more! I decided not to enlighten her about just how many teenagers had come and gone in our household, my own included, because it wasn't worth the argument. And besides, she'd probably have a quickfire response to that too. Instead, I had no choice but to allow her to leave the house, but with a tacit reminder that I still had my job to do. That, like it or not, she was a looked-after child and the 'looking-after' bit didn't just include me.

'So, it's Ryan now, is it?' I confirmed before she left. 'Just so I know, so I can add it to my daily reports. It's important I get it right. For the record.'

Elise rolled her eyes at me. 'Yes, it's Ryan. As in R.Y.A.N. Though I don't see why the social have to know my every move. It's not like they can do anything about it, anyway. Just nosey, if you ask me, and it's a bit weird, don't you think? A male social worker wanting to know the ins and outs of who I might be sleeping with. All a bit freaky, a bit *pervy*, don't you think?'

And there it was, that veiled threat, this time towards Graham. I made a mental note to include this conversation in my notes so that he was aware of it. It was things like this, things that could so easily be missed, that I needed to get down on paper in order to protect everyone. It was a horrible feeling, but dated conversations might be needed as evidence at some point and, as horrible as it felt, it had to be done.

I Just Want to be Loved

There were so many sides and layers to Elise that it was all too easy to become distracted, and often what you thought was happening, really wasn't, but because she was so convincing, so seemingly upfront and believable when she was telling you what she was doing, it always came as a shock when it transpired that it had all been a complete lie.

In fact, take the E and the S from her name and there you had it. The following morning, there I was feeling happy that Elise had decided that Ryan wasn't for her after all, when it all started to crumble with one single text message – to me, sent from up in her bedroom. A text I only saw some twenty minutes after she'd sent it, as I'd been out in the garden putting washing on the line.

I'm so scared, Casey, these girls on their way to ours and they're truly horrible! Nasty bitches who have said they're going to beat me up because apparently this Gemma Daley was going out with Ryan and I swear I didn't know! He really played me and I was too stupid to see it, and now all these sixteen-year-olds are coming to get me, please tell them I'm out, pleeeeeeaase!

I was just about to run upstairs to demand a full explanation when a loud banging at the front door caused me to stop, take a deep breath and prepare myself for whatever was to come.

'Can I help you?' I asked, smiling benignly at the teenagers standing on my path. There were five of them in total, three girls and two boys, all with the sort of expressions I'd seen about a million times before – part pugnacious, part swagger, part ever so slightly anxious about facing up to a stern-looking middle-aged woman. If I'd been asked to guess, I'd have said they were all around fifteen or sixteen. But not in uniform and not in school either. 'Is it Elise you want?' I continued, before any ventured to speak. 'Only she's in her room as she's feeling a bit unwell today, so, I'm sorry, but she's not coming out.'

That wasn't that far off the truth, I told myself, because, from the text message she'd sent, I guessed she probably *was* feeling a little sick at the moment, knowing (no doubt listening to) what was transpiring beneath her.

One of the girls, the oldest by the look of her, stepped forward. 'We don't want any trouble, and we know she's in care cos her parents are dead and stuff, but you should know she's bad news, lady, and you probably don't know the half of it.'

I filed away 'dead and stuff', to add to my notes. 'I'm sorry,' I said, smiling, 'but I can't discuss anything with you guys. I'm sure you understand, but I sincerely hope that there won't be any trouble. Elise is trying hard to fit in, and …'

I didn't get to finish my sentence as one of the boys suddenly burst out laughing. 'That's kinda the point. She's been fitting in just about everybody!'

The others then all started to laugh too. I glared at the older girl, the one who'd first spoken. 'Is that it? Is that all you came round for?'

She pushed her chest out. 'Look, there won't be any trouble if she stays away from our boyfriends. Tell her Gemma called and that if I find out she's been back to Ryan's flat, I won't be just giving her a warning.' She pointed to one of the other girls and added: 'I can't stop Sienna starting with her. That's up to her. But she slept with Matty on a fucking football field, and him and Sie have been together for six months! Elise is a dirty skank and someone will end up teaching her a lesson, so I'm just here to warn you. You're her foster mum, so you should know what she's up to.'

Well, that was true enough, certainly. Though as I watched them all march back down the front path I wondered what she'd meant. Did she think she was doing me a favour telling me, or was she implying that as a responsible foster carer I should know Elise's every move? Either way, I felt deflated as I closed the door and started to make my way upstairs, not least because, sadly, I believed what they'd told me. The truth was that I knew nothing about what Elise got up to when she wasn't at home. Or, rather, only knew what she told me, which could be – probably was – as far from the truth as her assertion to her peers that she was an orphan.

Still, there was one thing I could do and that was let her know how I felt. Not least about the fact that she'd brought those teenagers to my door, despite my making it clear that she must not give her so-called 'friends' our address.

She was sitting cross-legged on her bed and blowing her nose into a tissue when I got up there. 'Please, Casey, I don't want to talk about it,' she said. She plucked another tissue from the box on her bedside table and wiped her eyes with it. 'Thank you for stopping them, though. I was just so, so, so *scared*, I can't *tell* you.'

I tried to square her fear with the bunch of kids I'd just seen on my doorstep. Yes, they were lairy and bull-ish, but they were still basically kids. But then, I wasn't a fourteen-year-old, was I? And Elise was, which made half of me want to cross the room and comfort her, tell her that all was well and that we could indeed discuss it later, but the other half, the half that had just been confronted at my own front door, was having absolutely none of that.

'Well, I'm sorry, Elise, but if you're big enough for a whole lot of other grown-up things, you're most certainly big enough to get this straightened out right now. I can see you're upset and, of course, I'm not surprised, but I specifically told you not to tell your friends where we live, and you did. So, we are going to have this conversation whether it makes you uncom-fortable or not.' I sat on the stool at her dressing table and waited.

She sighed heavily. 'What do you want me to say?' she answered, her voice high and plaintive. 'Yes, I'm a slag? Yes, they're all telling the truth?' So, she'd either been listening or knew exactly what she was in their sights for. 'Because that's not the truth,' she went on.

'They're all liars! Okay, yes, Ryan was a genuine mistake. I never knew about Gemma until I'd already slept with him, then he just tossed me aside and told me I'd better keep it quiet because his girlfriend would go apeshit. He was using me, so of *course* I felt bad – and not just for me – for *her*. So, I added her on Facebook and told her what happened. See? *This* is what I get for being an honest person!'

The words all tumbled out so quickly that I was struggling to keep up. But when I did, it all figured, right down to her justification for the chaos she'd caused. 'And Matty?' I asked, keeping my voice low. 'Was he also a genuine mistake?'

Elise untangled her legs and drummed her fists on the bed. 'That never happened! Oh my God, I heard every word those bitches said and they're liars! I've only ever seen that Matty once and he was *with* Sienna when I did. They're just trying to shit-stir – trying to get you to chuck me out and it's all because their boyfriends fancy me. That's what all this is, can't you *see*? They want me out of the area so I'm not a threat to them. Jesus, this town is full of nasty skanks!'

Having heard enough – more than enough – I held a palm up. 'Elise, stop,' I said. 'I can't tell you which friends to choose or which boyfriends to have, because you'll go right ahead and do what you want anyway. All I can do is advise you, and my advice is that you give some serious thought to how close you came to having some real trouble on your hands today. Think what might have happened if that little group had confronted you out on the streets. Then I suggest you be a little bit more selective about who you hang around with. Please, Elise, *think*. You are better than this, sweetie. You have so much potential, and I just want you to be happy here, don't you see?'

To my surprise, Elise leapt from her bed then and came to hug me, smelling sweetly of coconut shampoo. 'I'm so sorry, Casey. I never should have allowed trouble at your door, I know that. I swear I'm going to stay in till all this blows over and I promise I will make some new friends.'

'Well, I hope so, for your sake,' I told her as she released me. 'And if all goes well tomorrow, you'll be in school next week anyway, where you'll definitely meet some new friends to hang around with and be able to let this lot go. But you know, love,' I added. 'This isn't just about those kids. It's about what *you* get up to. The things *you* do and say. I'm not going to go into the whys and wherefores of all this but you are old enough to understand that sleeping with boys you hardly know is a sure-fire recipe for trouble. You have agency, Elise, and you need to take some responsibility for yourself and your choices. Just because lots of boys fancy you, and I'm sure they do, doesn't automatically mean you are disliked by every girl you meet. Unless –' I took her hands here to try and really press my point home, 'you do something to give them good cause to. Do you understand what I'm saying?'

She nodded. 'I do. I don't mean to cause trouble. Honestly, I don't. I just ...'

'What, love?' I asked, as the silence began to lengthen.

'I just ... I just want ... I don't know. I just ... girls just don't *like* me. But boys ...'

Another silence. 'Boys do. Is that what you're saying? That boys do?'

'*Exactly*,' she said, wide-eyed, hands held out in supplication. 'So, what am I supposed to *do*?'

It was the way Elise had said that, as much as the words, that brought it home to me when I sat down with my laptop to write my notes up later. She just didn't get what I'd been saying to her. Not really. Whether consciously or unconsciously, she had a strong sense of herself as a victim – of the beauty she knew she possessed. And the belief that she was utterly powerless in the face of it, destined always to attract unsolicited male attention. And perhaps she *was* powerless, because she *needed* that attention. Needed that affirmation to shore up her self-worth. Looking for love, and in all the wrong places. It was the first proper glimpse I felt I'd had into her deeper psyche. Her seeming compulsion to 'conquer' every boy she encountered, and to hell with any girl that got in her way.

It was a lot to unravel, though on the face of it the root seemed obvious. Years and years of abandonment and rejection. But how to address it before she got into serious trouble? That was the bigger, more urgent, question.

Chapter 9

I don't know what it is about seeing a child for the first time in a new school uniform that has me reaching for my phone to take a snap, but it gets me every time. I just can't resist it. They always look so smart and cute and innocent, and, as Elise gave me a 'twirl' in hers, she looked all of those things. And amen to that. Perhaps we could now, at last, make some progress.

'Oh, Casey!' she scolded. 'I didn't know you were taking a photo. I wasn't ready!'

'You look amazing, sweetheart,' I said, feeling quite emotional. 'Just perfect.'

It had, thankfully, been a productive few days. The school meeting had gone smoothly – we were in and out within half an hour, Elise giving such a good account of herself that I could tell the head was wondering if this could possibly be the same girl he'd been briefed about, who'd been expelled – and with Graham offering to take her into town to get her uniform, I even enjoyed the luxury of a couple of hours with my youngest grandson that afternoon.

I also felt Elise was genuinely embracing it. Yes, it might have been that she stayed in all weekend for fear of bumping into certain people, but she'd thrown herself wholeheartedly into looking through some of the curriculum notes she'd been emailed by the school, and that was certainly good enough for me.

She reached out her hand for my phone now. 'Here, give it to me. Just for a sec. Let me take a couple of selfies for you – ones you'll like.'

And as I handed over my phone, the sentimental moment was over, though I couldn't help but laugh as she strutted around the living room, phone held above her head, pouting her lips and sucking in her cheeks. It never ceased to amaze me how adept kids were at taking photos of themselves – I'd yet to master holding a phone and pressing the button with the same hand. I couldn't even text with my thumbs yet.

And perhaps I never would be able to, either. 'Come on then,' I said as Elise finally finished her impromptu session. 'Let's go. We can't have you going in late on your first day.'

She had tried her best since the previous afternoon to get me to allow her to go by herself, saying she knew exactly how to get there as she'd done a 'dummy run' to get used to it. 'It's so lame being taken to school at my age,' she'd moaned. 'I'll be a laughing stock right from the start!'

But, as I'd kept reminding her, I'd been *told* to accompany her the first day. There were papers to be signed, agreements and medical authority forms and so on. So that was exactly what I would be doing. Besides, for all her apparent enthusiasm for starting back in school, half of me (well, a bit more than half, if I was honest) could not allow me to trust the evidence of my eyes in that regard. I would believe she was in school only when I left her there.

The journey to school was short and, mercifully, in the other direction to the rush-hour traffic – a big plus. It was one I'd made many, many times, back in the day, and once we'd arrived and had begun going through all the introductions to the teachers and office staff, I found myself thinking back to when I worked at this very school. If someone had asked me to describe the perfect student, then this version of Elise would have been it. Shy smiles, beautiful manners and so eloquent when answering questions. She never interrupted anyone and looked suitably thrilled and interested when the merits of the school were being spoken about. She even hugged me tightly before I left. 'Go on, Casey,' she told me, 'you enjoy your free time, and don't worry about me, I'm going to be perfectly fine here. It seems lovely.'

So far so good, then. I even caught the 'Oh, bless!' looks on the faces of the staff who had seen this exchange. But as I went back through the electric glass doors and into the car park, I could already feel my mood start to change. I didn't know why, but I just felt as though none of this was real; that Elise was directing a game that we were all playing, but one that we didn't know the rules to. Was this right? In reality, were all the adults in Elise's life simply pawns, waiting for her next move?

I tried to shake these absurd thoughts away as I drove back home to get cleaned up. Christine Bolton was calling to do a supervision visit, and I still had the breakfast dishes in the kitchen sink.

In social services, every few months, everyone has supervision with their manager, all the way up the line to the top staff, and this included the foster carers. First and foremost, it was an opportunity for line managers to check that everyone was doing their jobs correctly, but also to go over any problems that had been encountered. We would discuss how we had dealt with it, reflect on the outcome, and then go over how we might have handled it differently.

At first, these meetings had seemed a bit of a box-ticking exercise to me, but as the years passed I began to see the value of this kind of reflection, and each supervision left me with a renewed sense of purpose. The line manager would also remind staff of all the achievements, and all the little milestones that had been reached with a child, so all in all it was a very positive experience, and one which these days I looked forward to. Foster carers, in my opinion, do need this. They often feel adrift and alone in the day-to-day stuff, and supervision reinforces the fact that, actually, everyone above them is aware of all of it, and though there's no actual prize, the reward is simply knowing this.

My supervision wasn't technically due for another couple of weeks, but Christine had phoned me a couple of days earlier to give me some news.

'A huge box has arrived in the office, and apparently it contains the rest of Elise's things,' she said. 'Usually it would be Graham that brings it across – he collected it from Elise's grandmother's house – but he's on leave this week and it's been sitting here for a couple of days. I know your supervision visit isn't quite due yet but I thought I'd kill two birds with one stone and fetch it across. Is that alright?'

'Oh, that would be great,' I said, genuinely happy to be seeing Christine, not least because a few days earlier she'd emailed me with the news that her elderly father-in-law had passed away. He'd been very frail, and by this time completely lost to dementia, and though I knew that, in reality, it would have been a relief and a release, I still wanted to give her a hug. I knew Elise would be pleased to have her stuff too. 'She's been going on and on about having nothing to wear,' I said, 'so this will make her very happy indeed.'

It had. I'd promised Elise that her belongings would be there waiting for her when she got back from school and, as I suspected, she was very excited.

'You can help me unpack it, Casey,' she said, 'so no peeking until I get back. Oh, you're going to love, love,

love some of my outfits! You can borrow some if you like. I've got a couple of tops that would really suit you.' And though I'd laughed at the thought of wriggling into one of her skimpy crop tops, I was touched by the thought that Elise though they'd suit me and her sweet generosity in wanting to share.

And it turned out there was quite a lot of it, too. I opened the front door to find Christine half hidden by an enormous box and, judging by her groans, a pretty heavy one too.

'Everything bar the kitchen sink, I think,' she observed as I helped her manhandle it inside. 'Actually, scrub that. I think there must be a kitchen sink in there too. Either that or a set of encyclopaedias. Lord, what a weight!'

Having cajoled the box – more like a steamer trunk – to the bottom of the stairs together, I went to make her a restorative coffee. 'How are you doing?' I asked. 'I'm so sorry about your father-in-law.'

She shook her head briskly. 'Really, don't be. He had a good life, and a long one, and truth be told, it's a blessing. He'd have hated to see himself like that – wouldn't any of us? Anyway, how are you, more to the point? How have things been?'

That was typical Christine, pragmatic to a fault. And I had to agree; the thought of my kids having to watch me or Mike being swallowed up by dementia was one that gave me the shudders. And she was right. Wouldn't any of us feel the same? Yes, of course we would. And best not to dwell.

'Up and down,' I said. 'As you'll have seen if you've managed to catch up with my reports.'

'Not as much as I'd have liked to,' she admitted, 'what with the funeral arrangements and everything. But I'm not tight for time today, as a meeting just got cancelled, so how about we whizz through the supervision stuff, then you can properly give me chapter and verse. First up, though, how are the wedding plans going?'

Naturally, I had plenty to say about *that*. Though it was still over six months away, my brain had been busy whirring, and though I wasn't yet allowed to wade in with my suggestions, that hadn't stopped me planning in my head. So, what with that, and a general catch-up, and the supervision part of the visit, almost an hour had passed before we got on to the subject of Elise, starting with the feeling that had come over me earlier, that sense of being subtly, but constantly, manipulated by her; that despite the flashes of connection I felt with her here and there, that I shouldn't – no, didn't – believe anything the girl said, or, if I did, was always wondering about her motivation.

'Which makes me feel dreadful,' I said. 'Because it's so obvious from what I know of her background that she's a girl who could really use someone in her corner.'

'Interesting choice of word, "use",' Christine responded with a smile. 'I remember Jan saying much the same. Though in a different context, obviously. She said her mind told her one thing and her eyes something else. She very much felt, looking back, that Elise didn't want help – just a place from which to operate, someone to attend to her basic needs. But you are right, of course. She's clearly in need of a great deal more than that. Are you beginning to make any inroads in terms of working out what makes her tick?'

Christine clearly – and understandably – hadn't had much time to read my daily emails. 'Sex, on the face of it,' I told her. 'I know you warned me that she was sexually active, but she's also promiscuous. And quite astonishingly upfront about it, as well.'

I filled Christine in on what I'd heard and seen and felt in the last few days, plus my thinking about what might be driving Elise's behaviour, and her relentless seeking out of older boys. And with no care, apparently, whether they were already attached, much less the danger, or potential consequences of her actions. 'I can only hope school is going to help in that regard,' I said. 'It will at least stop her meeting up with all these older teenagers and fingers crossed also means she mixes with kids more her own age. I was also wondering, might there be a chance of contact with her grandmother on the horizon? I'm assuming she's out of hospital now?'

Christine nodded. 'Yes, I imagine she is. And as soon as Graham is back in the office next week I'll try to find out what's going on there. If anything,' she added, sighing. 'You know how things are. Ever-rising case numbers and way too few staff to spread the load.'

I did know, but after Christine left and my load of laundry and housework grew progressively lighter, my mood, I found, began to lighten with it. It was probably in part because I'd finally had a day to myself, but I found I was actively looking forward to Elise coming home, to helping her unpack her long-awaited possessions, and perhaps, as a consequence, even opening up a bit more about her gran. Even her parents.

Then I checked myself. That was possibly a little too Pollyanna-ish, but I was definitely looking forward to hearing all about what kind of day she'd had at school. Not least because I had such a great loyalty to it, and knew just how much being there could do for her.

'So, how did it go?' I asked the minute she stepped through the door. 'Did you make some new friends? Did you get lost in all the corridors? It took me weeks to find my way around when I was first there.'

Elise rolled her eyes as she shrugged her laden backpack from her shoulders. 'At least give me a minute to catch my breath!' she said, laughing. 'And get a drink. It's so sweaty in all this stuff and I'm absolutely parched. This blazer is, like, *so* hot!'

'So why didn't you take it off?'

'Because then I'd have to carry it, and have you felt the weight of this?' she added, handing me the backpack to demonstrate. 'And can you believe I got given homework on my first *day*?'

We went into the kitchen, and as I made her a glass of squash she rattled on about what she'd done and the other kids she'd met and the many delights the newly refurbished school canteen had to offer – all music to my ears. All so normal!

'By the way, that box in the hallway,' I said when she'd drawn breath. 'That's all your stuff. Christine Bolton dropped it over earlier today.'

'*Yesss!*' Elise said. 'So, my gran must be out of hospital. Can we go and unpack it now before tea?'

I glanced at the clock. It would be almost two hours before Mike and Tyler were home, so plenty of time to start prepping food. 'Course we can,' I said, smiling. 'Let's get the behemoth upstairs, then.'

'What's a behemoth?'

'A very big thing or creature. You wait till you try to shift it. Was collecting rocks ever a hobby of yours?'

We both laughed as we hauled the huge box up the stairs, but it wasn't long before any trace of humour was completely gone – at least on my part – as she started pulling out her items one by one.

First out were her clothes, which, in large part, were exactly as expected. Tiny tops, lots of T-shirts, skinny jeans and skimpy mini-skirts. 'Oh my God!' she cried, pressing a scrap of lace to her chest. 'I've missed these. They look so good with low-waisted jeans.' Out came another, then a third, then a fourth. Not scraps of lace but lace bodysuits, with thongs at the bottom, which would leave very, very little to the imagination.

She either didn't see me gape or it simply washed over her. 'You know you can borrow any of these

97

anytime, just help yourself. Oh, and this!' she then added, plucking out what looked like a satin basque. I didn't think I'd seen a basque for twenty years, much less the teeny scraps of underwear she was piling up beside it, none of which would have looked out of place in a bordello.

I tried to stop my eyes widening but it was getting increasingly harder. And it seemed there was another shock in store. She pulled out a bag then, a bulky one, and grinned as she peered in and looked at the contents. 'Top drawer for these, I think,' she said, with a smirk – before proceeding to decant half a dozen sex toys into the dresser.

So it seemed she *did* have a collection of sorts in there. Completely lost for words now, I said nothing whatso-ever. I mean, what did you say to a fourteen-year-old who's told you she's sexually active and thinks nothing of an adult witnessing her collection of vibrators?

I was therefore happy to be given an immediate distraction in the form of an old biscuit tin, gaily deco-rated with snow scenes, which she pulled up and handed across to me.

'What's this?' I asked.

'My keepsakes. Bits and bobs and stuff. Photos. Take a look if you like.'

'You sure? Isn't it private?'

She shook her head. 'Nah. It's just certificates and bits. Nothing that interesting. But you might like the photos. There's some of my little sister in there.'

I Just Want to be Loved

This was the first time I'd ever heard her mention her half-sister. So, this was a tiny chink of light that I could perhaps work with.

I was just about to ask her what her little sister's name was when she squealed, 'Baby bunny! I thought I'd lost her!' She hugged a tatty plush pink rabbit to her chest. And in much the same way, I couldn't help but notice, that she'd hugged the lace bodysuits to her minutes earlier. And thinking about what I'd witnessed her placing in the top of the dresser, I couldn't help but feel sickened. If you ever wanted a metaphor for loss of innocence, it was this. From a toy rabbit to sex toys in the blink of the proverbial eye. It felt almost inexpressibly sad.

Once again, as she placed the rabbit tenderly on her pillow, I reached for distraction in the form of the tin. It felt a little invasive to be opening it but at the same time I was glad – had she not invited me up to help her with the unpacking how many vital insights might have been missed?

I began leafing through the paperwork that comprised most of the contents, which, as she'd said, were pretty workaday things. Dentist and doctor appointments. A couple of swimming certificates. A class award from year four for 'good listening'. There were also leaflets from theme parks, a ticket stub from a cinema, plus a couple of pretty shells.

'From a trip to the seaside?' I asked, holding up the treasure.

She shook her head. 'Nah, just the shop at the Sealife Centre. We went on a school trip. It was peng.'

I wondered if she'd ever been to the seaside, but didn't ask her. Instead, I turned my attention to the raggy brown envelope at the bottom of the box, which was folded in half and presumably contained the photos. I was right. There were a dozen or so, the first of them typically emotive – a primary school class photo, a Halloween scene with Elise dressed as a witch, and a picture taken on what looked like a picnic, of a six- or seven-year-old Elise and, presumably, her father. Then one of a pretty dark-haired little girl, of maybe two or three.

Still on my mission to exploit this unexpected opportunity, I was just about to ask her about the photos – she was busy putting clothes in the dresser now – when I spotted a small cellophane pack of photographs still in the bottom of the tin, which I opened, and which instantly made my stomach churn. There were four of them, all taken at the same time, and I couldn't stop staring at them. They were of Elise, at around eight or nine, I'd guess, her hair styled into blonde ringlets, pouting and looking directly at the camera. Nothing unusual in that, necessarily, not given today's youth – indeed, at first glance, they had something of a Shirley Temple feel. But something about them screamed *wrong, wrong, wrong, wrong*. The red lipstick, for one thing, the white frilly knickers, the cropped bra-like top, and the way she was standing. She had a finger to her lips, as if shushing the photographer, and her bottom was sticking up and out suggestively. This was no little girl playing dress up. She'd been posed like this. By an adult.

The grim implications immediately obvious, my internal alarm bells began ringing overtime. I held the pictures up and, as lightly as I could, asked, 'How old were you in these, love? Who took them?'

She glanced across at the image and her eyes suddenly narrowed. I had the distinct impression she had forgotten they were there. Or that she thought she'd hidden them away better?

'That's in the past,' she said, taking the cellophane-wrapped pictures and the other photos too, then stuffing everything back in the tin, which she also took from me. I watched in silence as she pushed the tin far back beneath her bed.

'That's absolutely fine, love,' I said as she straightened. 'But if you do ever want to talk, then –'

'I don't,' she said firmly. 'Anyway,' she added, fixing a smile back in place, 'I'm done here. Shall we go down and start on tea? I'm starving.'

Sensing this was not the time to push it, I pasted a smile on too, but as I followed her down the stairs, the memory of the images only sharpened. And at least one aspect of Elise seemed to fall into place – a light had been shone on a childhood that it now seemed highly probable had been even more darker than we already knew.

Trauma in childhood has a severe impact in later life, and I knew now that this (whatever 'this' was, but the images seemed unequivocal) was probably the root of all of Elise's strange, highly sexualised behaviours. There was a great deal more to know, and though she clearly wasn't ready yet, she would have to confront it all at some point, for her future wellbeing. And maybe that was going to be my job here.

But would I dare to push and demand that she opened up her soul to me? It was a high-risk strategy. I knew from long experience that it would mean walking a fine line; I might end up pushing her further away. But if I *did* want to make a difference, I would have to.

Chapter 10

I was itching to get Elise off to school the next morning, mainly so that I could phone Christine to tell her about the contents of the biscuit tin and the images I'd seen, but also so I had space to really think and try to plan how to get the girl to talk about her past to me. I thought I might phone Riley – she was really good at this sort of thing, and when I hit a brick wall, or couldn't see the wood for the trees, she would often come up with a simple solution that I hadn't thought about.

Elise, however, was in no such rush. 'Any chance of a bacon sandwich this morning, please, Casey? Pretty please? I don't really fancy cereal today.'

I dragged out the frying pan and started to cook with one eye on the wall clock, and trying to work fast. Elise was walking to school today with a new friend (already!), so she'd have to set off soon. Bacon indeed!

'Here you go,' I said, thrusting the sandwich at her finally, 'but if your friend comes to the door you'll have to eat it on the way, love. You can't be late on your second day there.'

Right on cue, the doorbell rang, and after wrapping the uneaten bacon sandwich in a square of foil, I ushered Elise down the hallway. 'Chop, chop,' I said, 'and don't get bacon grease on that blazer. It's a bugger to get out.'

Elise laughed. 'God, Casey, what *is* with you this morning? I've got loads of time to get there. Stop fussing!'

It was such a normal conversation to have with a fourteen-year-old that, to an observer, such as the smiling girl who was now on the doorstep, things couldn't seem more normal. But the images I'd seen still stuck fast to my retina. 'It's my job,' I said, smiling back at her and pushing Elise through the doorway. 'Hi, I'm Casey,' I said. 'I'm sorry, Elise did tell me your name, but I've forgotten already.'

'Oh, how embarrassing!' Elise said dramatically as she flounced past me. 'Come on, Serenity, let's go before she really shows me up.'

Serenity. That was it. No such state of mind for me currently. I watched the girls walk up the street before going back inside, back to my constantly racing thoughts. I felt sorry for poor Mike, as I hadn't slept at all well; I knew I'd woken him up at least three times with my constant tossing and turning, as I'd tried to stop my brain working overtime. I'm one of those people who struggles to keep my eyes open while watching a movie before bed, but the minute I get into the bedroom, my brain starts tormenting me. Some of my night-time Google searches would perplex a psychologist for sure: 'What time is it now in Atlanta?' 'Do frogs sleep?' 'Tell me about the Big Bang.' I have no idea why these bizarre things pop into my head when the lights go off, but they do – and when I'm fretting about a particular foster child, I'm even worse.

Christine was in a meeting when I rang her, so it was getting on for eleven before I could connect with her and tell her what I'd found the previous afternoon. Perhaps *un*surprisingly, she didn't sound surprised at all.

'Well, we've always thought some kind of sexual abuse may have occurred when she was younger,' she said, 'and what you describe certainly would go along with that theory, but you know, most kids wouldn't want to be reminded of something like that, would they? It does sound very strange.'

'So, I haven't stumbled across some great mystery then,' I said. 'I mean, the story is that she has been abused, is that what you're saying? Because, yes, if that's a fact, then you're right, it's very strange that Elise would want to keep a visual reminder of the time. Has it ever been proven?'

'No, it never was, and again, that's partly Elise's fault. Over the years she has partly opened up to teachers, friends and parents of friends, apparently. But it appears that just as any investigation was started, the girl would act as if it was all a big joke and say it never happened – that she just wanted to get her mum or dad or whoever into trouble. And as far as we can tell from the information we've been given, every alleged abuser has always strongly denied anything happened and, because there was never any evidence to support her claims, all investigations ceased at that point.'

I'd have loved to have had sight of the whole dossier, so I could see the bigger picture. There was clearly information going years back about Elise. But, as ever, the big frustration was that there would not be a comprehensive file as such. Though information sharing starts happening as soon as a child enters the care system – collated school records, doctors' notes, hospital admissions, any police records that may be in existence – no central file on a child ever seems to be created. So things get missed. Sometimes important things, and sometimes for years.

'But what about the photos?' I asked. 'Aren't they evidence?'

'Well, I haven't seen them, obviously, and from how you describe them, they are enough to make your skin crawl, but real evidence? I doubt they are on their own. Elise would have to be able to tell someone about the circumstances surrounding the pictures, and if she was very young at the time, well, I don't suppose she'd really remember, do you?'

'Not *that* young.'

'No, you're right. But if Elise had wanted to corroborate them she could have – and hasn't. And, so far, won't. For whatever reason. I mean, the feeling is that

Elise *has* actually been abused, but without anything concrete …'

She allowed the words to trail and I could feel my heart sinking in increments as Christine spelt it out to me. Something wasn't right about those photographs – they would make anyone recoil – and surely someone in authority needed to at least look at them? If nothing else they would be on file, and perhaps might be useful going forward.

I told Christine I was still going to try to encourage Elise to talk to me about her past, and that I felt it was important that she start to confront her demons. Well, assuming she even recognised that there were demons to be confronted, and, as things stood, I wasn't sure she even did. Not consciously, at any rate.

'I agree, absolutely,' Christine said. 'And in that regard, there's something else. I was just about to call you anyway. As much as I hate to add to your stress, it seems there's been another incident. Elise is to be allocated a new social worker. A female one. Graham is refusing to see her anymore.'

The heartsink feeling intensified, as I predicted what was coming. 'So what happened?' I asked. 'Another false allegation? Against him?'

'Not that I'm aware of, and she's presumably said nothing to you, but he feels – and very strongly – that she was putting down a marker. It was after the school visit, when he drove her into town to pick up some uniform, and she apparently dropped her phone in his footwell.' I heard her sigh. 'I mean, *really*? How could anyone in a passenger seat *accidentally* drop a phone in the driver's footwell? Plus, he was driving at the time, too, so there wasn't much he could do when she leaned across and put her arm down beside his leg to retrieve it. Which wouldn't have been so bad, were it not for the fact that she giggled as she picked it up, her forearm brushing his leg, and apparently said, "Don't worry, I won't tell if you won't." I mean, what was the poor man supposed to make of that? Anyway, he told her to behave herself but of course it preyed on him all night. Effectively, just as is the case with your Tyler, he realised he was a sitting duck if ever he was on his own with her. And she was, in his opinion – and I have to agree – making that very point. To what end, I have no idea, but there it is. They are going to bring in someone new as soon as they can.'

'Well, I can't say I blame him,' I said. 'I just wish I could better understand why she does it. Is it a vendetta against men? Or is it just to make mischief for attention?'

'Possibly a bit of both,' Christine said. 'But either way, you'll need to tread carefully. And I have to tell you that, from now on, Elise is never to be left alone with any of the males in your family, including Mike and Tyler. Which I know is going to put added pressure on the placement, because it's always going to have to be you that transports her anywhere. You'll have to be sure you don't take a bath or go to the shops or anything and leave her wandering around where Mike or Ty are. It's just too risky. Is that going to be possible? I know it's difficult.'

Difficult was an understatement. It was going to put huge pressure on our household, and once again I found myself wondering if we'd made a huge mistake in continuing with Elise. Especially when she seemed so hell-bent on making it that way.

That said, however, Tyler was pretty much doing that in any case – he'd been spending a lot more time at Naomi's than home since Elise had arrived, and I knew full well that the two things weren't unrelated. And as for Mike, well, we were always hyper-careful when it came to teenage girls generally, for exactly that reason. Yes, Mike had often done lifts into town while I made dinner, or taken a girl to her friend's house, but it wasn't such a big deal that I'd do all the lifts with this one.

'Don't worry,' I reassured Christine. 'We can make it work.'

'I knew you'd understand,' she said, 'but there's just one more thing I need to tell you …'

One more thing. Honestly, she was like bloody Columbo! Surely there wasn't worse to come? There was.

'It seems that the reasons behind Elise's school expulsion were deliberately vague,' Christine said, 'but we've managed to find out – well, actually your local school have, because the head there is friends with the head at Elise's old school – that she was expelled for seducing a twelve-year-old boy, on the school grounds, and encouraging him to have sex with her. And before you ask, yes, there were several witnesses.'

Another incident, another image that almost beggared belief.

Except perhaps not that much. Thinking back to my very earliest days fostering, I couldn't help but be reminded of a pair of siblings we'd taken in. They'd both been sexually abused – horrendously so – but the older child was the one with the greater psychological damage. Abused almost since birth, sexual impropriety had become his 'normal', and behaving inappropriately with his little sister had too. Tragically, having already lost every single member of their family (several to lengthy prison sentences), the two children had had to be permanently separated, for their own good.

Were we seeing something similar at work here with Elise? Had sexual impropriety become almost a compulsion?

'Great,' I said, groaning. 'But how the hell is all this stuff not on her records?'

'It actually is when you set about looking for it,' Christine admitted. 'But for some reason none of it was included in her care plan. God knows why, but I promise you I'm looking into it. I mean it could just be clerical error, but that's no excuse.'

I knew from her tone that Christine felt guilty. She knew as well as I that, had I been in possession of the full facts at the outset, I might have thought twice about taking Elise on. But there was no point in crying over spilt milk. And, in truth, the more nuggets of information we unearthed about her past, the stronger my conviction became that this child needed urgent psychological help. Which I must press to be arranged for her. I said as much now. 'Well, if she can be persuaded to engage.'

'Well, at least in that respect, it's positive, as she's already in their system. Jan went through the same process, as you probably know, and even managed to get an initial meeting organised. But she point-blank refused to have anything to do with it. And, as you know …'

I sighed. 'No one can make her.'

And that was truly the bottom line. If Elise didn't want to accept help, no one could force her to do anything. In theory she could see out her time with us – however long that turned out to be – accepting nothing more than the everyday care we provided. A roof over her head, food in her tummy, security and companionship, and little more. In terms of making a difference – well, we really *could* end up being little more than that proverbial B & B. By the time I got off the phone to Christine, I was mentally shattered, with a throbbing pressure building at my temples. I ran a glass of water, then took two paracetamols to soothe my headache. There was a hell of a lot more to our girl than we'd first thought, and I had a hell of a lot more work ahead if I had any chance of helping her. Starting with clearing the first and highest hurdle. Getting her to believe, and to accept, that she even needed help.

Bite-sized pieces, Casey, I told myself as I reached for my laptop, opened Word and pulled up a blank page. I would type out everything I knew so far in the first section, then all my thoughts and suspicions in another. Then, finally, a list of things I could do in small steps to at least start trying to find some solutions for Elise. It was the only way I knew to organise my chaotic thoughts. Get it all down on paper and then stare at it for a while.

But it was like looking into a pit full of snakes.

Chapter 11

As worrying as the last few days had been, I could still feel some relief as I regained some of my freedom. The first week of school for Elise had seemingly gone really well. She was enjoying it and never once complained about getting up early or doing homework. Something to celebrate, I thought, especially for a girl who had been out of education for so long. So, partly because of how generous I was feeling, after having practically a full week to myself to go visit the kids and do some much needed retail therapy with the bride to be, and partly because I wanted Elise to feel like she had achieved something – which she had – I organised an impromptu family outing on the Friday night. A first big step on the road to integrating her with the wider Watson clan.

'Oh,' Elise said, frowning, when I made my big announcement. 'I *was* going to go out and meet some of my new mates tonight. Can we not do it tomorrow?'

Nothing like having the wind taken out of your sails. 'No, we blooming well can't,' I said, slightly chippily. 'I've already arranged everything. Mike's finishing work early, Ty and Naomi are meeting us at the restaurant, and so are Kieron and Lauren. I was hoping Riley and David would be coming too but they're stuck for a babysitter, so –'

'So it's okay for Riley to opt out, then?'

'Yes, but –'

'So why can't I? If it's a family affair anyway, I don't see why you need me to –'

'It's an outing arranged *for* you,' I interrupted, because two could play at that game. 'So you can get to know everyone a little better. That's the whole *point* of it, Elise, so I'm sorry, but you'll just have to let your friends know you're busy, and that you'll catch up with them over the weekend. Sweetheart,' I added, trying to hide my irritation at her apparent lack of interest in getting to know us better, 'it's to celebrate how well you've done at your first week in school. And it'll be fun.'

She frowned again but, perhaps sensing this was a done deal, she finally nodded. 'Okay. Sorry. I didn't realise. I'll go and message my mates, then,' she added, heading for the door to go up to her room. But then she seemed to have an afterthought. She turned back towards me. 'Thank you. I *am* grateful. It was just, you know, I'd already made plans, and I don't like letting people down.'

'I'm sure they'll understand,' I said, feeling the irritation rise again, both at the idea that I was forcing her to do exactly that, and that I was being a nuisance, interfering with her apparently much more important social life. But she was fourteen, I reminded myself, so I had to make allowances.

As did she, and I got the sense that she'd now thought that through. 'They'll be cool about it,' she agreed. 'Where are we going anyway?'

'A new Brazilian place in the town centre. I've heard some fab reviews about it. Apparently you pay one price and can eat as much meat and salad and stuff as you like.' I smiled at her. 'I've practically starved myself all day so I can take full advantage of it.'

'Sounds great,' Elise said, looking happier now as she turned to go upstairs. 'I'll wear jeggings so I can eat loads, then!'

I watched her go, wondering quite why she'd managed to rattle me the way she had and fixing, once again, on the way she seemed to see the placement. As if she was simply renting space – bed and board – in our family home, our comings and goings of little interest to her. *Us*, as a family, of little interest to her. Yes, she seemed to be settling in okay after the drama of the early days, but more as a lodger than a looked-after child. At least in her mind, I reckoned. But she was a child, and a vulnerable one, even if she couldn't see that. And one with an even darker past than we'd up to now imagined. I could only hope that Christine was successful getting help for her. And that I would have more luck than Jan in persuading her to engage with it.

But it was a problem closer to home that would be on my mind a couple of hours later.

The restaurant turned out to be as fun and unique as it had been billed. I've never been to Brazil, so I couldn't accurately attest to its authenticity, but as we settled down at our huge table, I was definitely impressed.

'I think you'd best close your mouth, Mum,' Kieron said, laughing at me as I stared all around, loving the bright colours and fancy bunting. 'A waiter might come around and stuff a lamb chop in it or something.'

I did as suggested, but only momentarily. I was buzzing. 'Oh, but just look at those gorgeous lampshades, and all that ivy round the beams! It's all so pretty here – it's like being plonked down in a favela or something.'

Lauren spluttered at this. 'A favela?' She grinned at me. 'Hardly!'

'Well, whatever. I like it. So, enlighten me, someone. How does it all work?'

In a complicated fashion, as it turned out. There were no menus, for a start. Just a list of everything available, which miraculously appeared on our table, one meat after another. Waiters, parading around with huge metal skewers containing cuts of different meats, simply shaved portions of it off onto every plate they saw. At some point, I must have looked aghast as yet more BBQ pork was piled onto my already full plate, because Mike nudged me as the others chatted.

'Turn your stick thing over to red,' he said, 'and they'll stop coming.'

'What? What stick thing?'

Mike reached across to my coloured wooden flag on a stick and flipped it, so that it was no longer green. 'Red means stop, green means keep it coming,' he explained.

Well! Someone could have told me! I thought my pretty flag was yet another Brazilian touch. Still, Mike was gracious enough not to spill his guts and have everyone laugh at me again.

It was a lovely evening, and the food was as delicious as billed, despite the enormous portions, and it made me so happy to see everyone getting along so well and including Elise in the family chit-chat. But at the same time, there was no denying it – I had this growing sense that something wasn't quite right with Ty. I couldn't place my finger on what, exactly – he and Naomi seemed as joined at the hip as ever – but now and then I just felt he looked slightly tense, and once or twice caught Kieron looking at him pointedly.

I couldn't ask either of them about it, however, as both were on the far side of the vast table. So, when Lauren said she was nipping off to the ladies' room, I tagged along too, my antennae suggesting they all knew something I didn't.

I waited till we'd both emerged from our respective cubicles. 'Sweetie,' I asked her, 'is everything okay with Ty?'

Washing her hands, as was I, she looked up at my reflection. And in such a way as to confirm my suspicions. She didn't look anxious, exactly, just slightly awkward. Then she frowned slightly. 'It's not really for me to say,' she said. Then, seeing my expression, 'Don't worry, Casey – it's nothing bad.'

So not an unexpected pregnancy. 'What, then?' I asked her. 'Can't you at least give me a hint?'

She looked back towards the door. 'To be honest, I thought he'd have already told you. He said he was going to – he and Naomi – but I guess he's not yet plucked up the courage yet, bless him.'

'Courage? What does he need courage for?'

Lauren frowned. Then seemed to decide. 'Look, you mustn't let on that I've told you this, but he and Naomi are planning to move to York at the end of this month.'

'What?' I said, stunned. 'What, both of them? And why this month? Naomi doesn't start uni till September. And why Ty too?' I added, it suddenly hitting home. *Hard.* They wouldn't be parted when she started her teacher training. He was going to move there as *well.* 'But where will they live?' I asked Lauren, my mind teeming with questions now.

She put her hands under the dryer, blasting the tiny room with noise. 'I think they've found somewhere – a flat,' she said, raising her voice above the din. 'But look, it should be *them* telling you all this. Not me.'

'Well, I'm glad you did,' I said, as the air flow finally ceased. 'Gives me time to compose myself.'

'*Exactly*,' she said pointedly. My daughter-in-law-to-be knew me well. 'And don't be too hard on him. I know he's been dreading breaking the news to you, as I'm sure you can imagine.'

But Tyler had now, it seemed, plucked up the courage, because when we returned to the table, I knew something had changed. Elise was scrolling through her phone now, having effectively exited whatever conversation they'd all been having – and they clearly had, because Tyler smiled at me nervously and Mike gave me a look that made it clear he was in on things now too. And I didn't have to worry about landing Lauren in it because as soon as she sat down she said, 'Don't worry, Ty. I've told Mum.'

I couldn't help it. 'York? *Now*?' I said. '*Both* of you? Why now? And what will you do for money? For work? Ty, what about your *job*?'

Mike raised his hand and smiled at them. 'Love, let the lad speak!'

Ty coloured. 'I'm sorry I haven't told you yet,' he said, squeezing Naomi's hand as he spoke. It was a sweet gesture but made me check myself, too. Was I really so scary that he'd been frightened about telling me? No, I decided, they were just showing solidarity. That they were a team, and what more could a mum want than that?

Tyler glanced nervously at Mike and then looked back at me. 'We're going to York tomorrow to sign the paperwork for a flat we like. We viewed it when we were there last.' He glanced at Naomi. 'And it looks like we've got it. We –'

'My dad's helped us out with the deposit,' Naomi added, answering my unspoken question. 'And we've been saving –' she glanced at Ty again. 'We've done all the sums. It's only small. Not too expensive … and Ty already has a potential second interview for a job, so …'

They had indeed done the sums, I thought, as they began sharing it all with us. Explaining how there were actually quite a few vacancies in the local leisure centres and how Naomi, too, was confident of getting employment there – full time over the summer and then part time during term time. How they'd realised they didn't want a long-distance relationship. How excited they both were about setting up home together. 'And it's not *that* far,' Tyler pointed out. 'We'll be able to come back loads.'

'And York's a nice place for a minibreak,' Mike pointed out to me.

And I agreed, even as my heart was lodged down in my summer sandals. *But why now?* I wanted to ask them. Why not wait until September? But I knew better than to ask that, so I didn't.

'You're not too angry are you, Casey?' Naomi asked, reading my clearly not-hidden-well-enough expression.

'No, no, of *course* I'm not angry, sweetheart,' I reassured her. 'I could never be angry about any of my kids flying the nest. I'm just, well, a bit stunned, I suppose. I just, well, I wasn't expecting it *now*. That's all.' I looked from one to the other and smiled. 'When I so obviously should have been, shouldn't I?'

'It just makes perfect sense to us, Mum,' Tyler said, leaning across the table to cover my hand with his. 'There are great opportunities there for me too. I can be close to Naomi, and I get to stand on my own two feet. Please say you're okay with it.'

I could see the sincerity and anxiety in his eyes. And the love. Which made my heart feel fit to burst now. 'Oh, Tyler,' I said, 'of course I'm okay with it, darling, and yes, you are right to want to stand on your own two feet, and I'm so proud of you for that.' I turned to Naomi. 'And you too, love, I'm so proud of you too. If either of you need any help, with anything, honestly, you have mine and Mike's full support. And the move, of course. On hand for everything and anything, basically.'

'Well,' said Mike. 'I think this calls for a celebration drink.' He raised a hand to flag down one of the waiters. 'Let's have some bubbles, to toast the big fledging.'

The big final fledging, I thought, tasting the bitter-sweetness, five minutes later, as the bubbles landed on my tongue. And the fact that something else was nagging at me too. Something I only got a chance to voice as we were leaving, and I had a moment alone with my youngest son.

'You sure you're okay with all this, Mum?' he asked me. 'I know it's come out of the blue for you but I didn't want to say anything till we were sure we could do it.' He gave me one of the old-fashioned looks I knew so well. 'Till I knew you wouldn't be able to talk me out of it, basically.'

'As if I ever would,' I said, digging him in the ribs. 'It's your life, and this is an exciting adventure. Just … one thing,' I asked, because it was beginning to really nag at me. 'Is your going now, as opposed to in the autumn, anything to do with Elise living with us? Because I swear, if it is, I can do something about that. I won't have anyone make you feel so uncomfortable that you feel you can't stay in your own home, love.'

Tyler hugged me. 'Mum, now you're being silly. That would never happen, and I know without a doubt that you'd never *allow* that to happen. If I'm being honest, then yes, maybe if Elise weren't there, maybe I'd have waited until September, and yes, perhaps her being at ours pushed us to make the move a bit sooner, but it's definitely not because of her. It's because we want to be together.'

I believed every word he said, and although it saddened me that this whirlwind of a girl had rocked our household enough that Tyler had brought forward his long-term plans, I realised that Elise was merely the catalyst. He was ready to be a grown-up and I had to accept it. Yes, he wasn't quite yet nineteen – still so *young* – but he'd been through so much in his short life that he had maturity beyond his years. And he was right. York really wasn't so far away.

'Don't be taking the wind out of our sails, mate,' Kieron joked as we climbed into our respective cars. He and Lauren were going to be dropping the lovebirds back to Naomi's. 'You two can have your moment of glory, but don't forget it's our wedding that will top the league table of big events this year.'

'Oh, don't worry,' Mike said, 'Casey won't let anyone forget about *that*.' He looked at Elise then, who was still detached, still scrolling through her phone. I wondered if she'd even cared that the evening had turned out, by its end, to not be much about her after all. 'You've no imminent announcements have you, love? Not getting engaged, married, divorced, moving out?'

Elise switched on her smile and pushed out her full belly. 'Just that I have the biggest food baby *ever*,' she said, grinning. 'And hey,' she added, almost as if the thought had just occurred to her, 'with Tyler gone, I'm going to be your only child, aren't I?'

At which everyone laughed, including me. But I was faking it. It wasn't so much what she'd said as the prospect itself. It gave me the strangest feeling of foreboding.

Chapter 12

By the middle of the following week, I think I had just about come to terms with the fact that Tyler was going to move out. It brought back memories of when Riley and then Kieron had left home, and although Tyler wasn't my biological child, this separation was going to affect me just as heavily. The whole family loved Ty, and he did us. We *were* family. I still remembered vividly the moment when it first struck me that I must keep him, that I must be the mother he so badly needed – the mum he had already confided he loved like a mum. I remembered too the conversation in my mother's kitchen when the scales fell from my eyes. 'So, *keep* him!' she'd commanded, while stirring eggs for an omelette, in response to my rationalising that I must be free to care for other kids. Which logic had told me I must, even as my heart was screaming otherwise; we'd been trained, at some expense, to be specialist carers, and to take Tyler on permanently would mean we'd be less able to take in the most challenging and troubled kids.

Looking back now, it was madness to even question that it was the right thing. That I'd doubted even for an instant that I should follow my heart.

And now, all these years later, the bittersweet time had come that must come for every parent. So much pride and joy and happiness, yet that hole in my heart. And another empty bedroom in the house.

You've still got Elise, I told myself sternly. *And there will always be other kids who need you to support them. So, it's not like you're going to be bored, is it?* I put the kettle on, spooned coffee into my mug and then turned up the radio, to drown out the feeling that accompanied the thought that, in terms of forging a relationship with this complicated girl, I had still made so little progress.

Enough, I decided. This was not a road to go down. I needed to do something productive, not wallow in maudlin thoughts. Elise was at school and seemingly getting on okay there, the house was all spick and span, and there were no cupboards to sort out – at least none that I was inclined to tackle – and I had an hour before I had to start making tea. So, fighting away the inevitable guilt, I grabbed my laptop from the small desk in the dining room, set my coffee on the side table and then stretched out on the sofa. Stuff it. I'd have some of what Riley called 'me time', catching up on my friends' and relatives' lives on Facebook. Which was productive in its own way, I reassured myself, as it would allow me to switch off from my own woes.

It had been a while, so I spent the first fifteen minutes or so catching up on all the notifications I'd received and then leaving the obligatory likes and laughing and sad faces as seemed appropriate. Truth be told, some of the stuff I scrolled through on Facebook often had me wondering why on earth there wasn't a rolling-eye emoji, but there wasn't, so I would ignore the kind of comments that would have had me doing that in real life and concentrated on friends' holiday snaps, on birthdays and on weddings, as well as all the inconsequential chatter and silly photos that constituted much of my news feed.

After catching up with my virtual world, I then turned to my messages. Predictably, after a gap of several days, I'd missed quite a few, and, as ever, I wondered if this really could be called progress because, back in the day, these would all have been phone calls or face-to-face chats – not a responsibility to regularly go, on my own, and check 'social' media, just in case. There was a three-day-old one from my sister, Donna, asking if I'd like to go to the cash and carry with her, and two from Mike, tagging me in some gardening equipment on the 'For Sale' pages, which he'd neglected to mention in person. There was also one from Kieron, asking me to let him know what colour outfit I was planning to wear to the wedding, so he could inform Lauren's mum, and we could 'maybe coordinate so you don't end up clashing?' The vision of two violently hued mothers-in-law giving everyone a migraine brought a smile to my face, even as I wondered why he hadn't just called me.

I then turned, as I usually did, to message requests, where people I might or might not know in real life, but wasn't 'friends' with on Facebook, could send me a message and wait for me to approve it. I knew from others that this often was a depository for missives from ne'er do wells and weirdos, but, in my case, more often than not they came from friends of friends of friends or, once or twice, from kids I'd fostered in the past. So, I made a point of checking pretty regularly.

Today's crop was tiny – just one single message. From someone called Emma Giles, whose name rang no bells. I clicked to open it – you could do that without the sender being aware of it – and a name jumped out at me immediately: Elise. *I've tracked you down as the parent of Elise Blackwell*, the message started. *And I hope you're proud of what she is. Thanks to her I've thrown my husband out. You should be ashamed of yourself that your daughter would do this, she's nothing but a little slag!*

To say I was shocked would be an understatement, and at first I didn't know what to do. The woman clearly knew Elise, but it puzzled me how she had tracked me down and connected me to her. But how to respond? There were strict protocols about who I could be clear with about our situation. Obviously, doctors, the police and anyone else in authority I knew I could be frank with, but I certainly wasn't allowed to discuss our foster kids with people generally, and definitely not on social media, but I did need to know what all this was about. After a couple of minutes gathering my thoughts, I began to type back. I said nothing about being a foster carer and not a parent. I simply asked if she could explain her message and then sat back to wait for a reply. Almost instantly, I saw the three flashing dots that showed me the person was replying, and it's a good job I didn't hold my breath as it seemed to go on and on forever. Finally, a huge message appeared, and as I started to read it, the now familiar heartsink sensation overtook me. What on earth did Elise think she was doing?

The lengthy message had obviously been written in anger and distress, and was peppered with capitals and expletives, the latter mostly aimed at Elise.

But it boiled down to a tale that, though it might seem far-fetched on the face of it, knowing Elise and some of the antics she'd been up to already, I just knew, almost certainly, would be true.

It had started several days back, it seemed, when Elise had contacted the woman's husband, seemingly randomly, on Facebook, and sent him a number of photographs of herself, all naked, and one using a sex toy. *I've seen them*, the woman railed. *And, believe me, they're DISGUSTING.*

But also tempting, apparently, because her husband had, unbelievably, continued the conversation, clearly flattered and titillated by this unexpected contact, and when Elise asked if he wanted to see more he had said yes.

I mentally reached for that imaginary eye-roll emoji. How could anyone be so stupid or naive? But then I checked myself. Perhaps it was me being the naive one. Pornography was everywhere, and these days the internet was the commonest gateway to obtaining it. This man was playing with fire, certainly, but it really *would* be naive of me to imagine he was a rarity. This sort of thing went on everywhere, every hour of every day.

Feeling my gloom deepen – why would she *do* this? – I read on. A few days had passed, apparently, then Elise sent a message to the woman who'd contacted me now, including said photos, plus screenshots of the conversations with her husband, and the message – which pinged into my inbox that very second – that 'your husband is a paedo!!! I am FOURTEEN years old!! Look what he's been doing with me online while you're in bed!!!!'

With the liberal use of exclamation marks, it sounded as juvenile as intended, even if Elise probably wouldn't see that herself. But *why* had she done it? Did she know this man in some way? What on earth would possess her to make such mischief otherwise? I needed answers – proper answers. Not the usual vague flim-flam. And I would seek them the very moment she came home.

In the meantime, I had to respond to this traumatised woman. Mindful of my position, and not knowing quite what to say to her, I typed a short message: *I'm so sorry about this. I don't really know what else to say other than to apologise. Elise isn't our child – we look after her – but I will pass on this information to her social worker.*

I knew I'd have to tell Christine Bolton about it, and also tell her how I'd responded. I hadn't gone into any details but I *had* indicated that Elise was a looked-after child. Given the situation, I didn't think I'd get into trouble for admitting this, but after thinking about it for a moment, I sent a second message saying that, unfortunately, I wouldn't be able to have any further correspondence with this woman, but that once again I was sorry. A reply came straight back: *Well, if you're looking after her, then you should be more vigilant about what she's getting up to! Thanks to her, my marriage is over and my daughter has lost her daddy, so tell that to the social worker as well!*

I felt sickened. I could only hope that wouldn't be the case. That they could find a way to work through it, and that the woman would forgive him. Perhaps understand the extreme temptation that had been placed before him and give him another chance. But would I? Hand on heart, would I do that if it were Mike?

Don't even go there, I thought, pushing the train of thought away. I knew nothing about these people, or their marriage, and it wasn't my job to speculate or philosophise about any of that. My job was to concentrate on the girl in my care, and stop this sort of thing in its tracks, because I had the strongest sense that this might not have been an isolated incident.

I Just Want to be Loved

But *did* she know the man? Was that it? Was he someone from her past? Was she righting some historical wrong? Avenging some past hurt or trauma? Might this be in some way connected to those photographs I'd seen? Because this was a mighty big leap from telling tales in the playground about adolescent boys. This was serious, potentially life-destroying stuff, and it was essential I got to the root of it all. Either way, be it a personal vendetta or just her 'new thing', I needed to take immediate action to nip it in the bud.

I logged off Facebook and slapped my laptop shut, then looked up at the clock. Which I would watch till she walked through the front door.

Chapter 13

I heard the front door open and jumped up immediately. My intention was to get Elise sitting down in the dining room, before she launched into a step-by-step résumé of her day, but it seemed our girl had other ideas.

'Hi, Casey!' she shouted from the hall. 'I'm not staying. I'm just nipping in to use the loo. Josh is with me and I said we'd walk down to the park for a bit. Meet up with some friends for a bit. That okay?'

I could hear the downstairs cloakroom door slamming shut as she shouted all of this, and as I stepped into the hall I almost bumped into a tall, skinny lad who was hovering by the front door, and who looked pleasingly much like any fourteen-year-old would at the end of the school day, shirt half hanging out, tie askew, shoes scuffed; i.e. the sort of lad I would be very happy to see Elise hanging out with in the park after school, just like any other group of teenagers on a summer afternoon.

But not right now, obviously. Typical! Why today, of all days?

'Hi, I'm Josh,' he said, dropping his head shyly as I met his gaze. 'Elise said to come in and wait?' he added, nodding to the still half-opened front door, and possibly tuning into the vibe I was giving off, that today wasn't actually the best day.

Now, here I had two choices. Be cool mum of the year, smile and make the lad feel welcome, then allow Elise to go out and leave my chat with her till later. Option two, of course, was to be the world's most annoying and embarrassing mother, send the boy on his way and insist that Elise remain in the house. No gold stars for guessing which I had to be, and as much as I knew it was the right choice, it gave me no gratification whatsoever.

'I'm really sorry, Josh,' I said, my voice lowered enough so that Elise wouldn't hear, 'but I'm afraid you're going to have to walk down by yourself. I have something I need to discuss with Elise, so she won't be going with you. I'll tell her to give you a call later on.'

'Oh, okay,' the boy said, looking nonplussed as he turned around and stepped back onto the doorstep. 'Tell her I said bye, then?'

'I will,' I assured him, quickly closing the door behind him, just as I heard the loo flush down the hallway. I then went back into the dining room to wait for Elise to reappear, which she did seconds later, wiping still-damp hands on her school skirt.

'Where's Josh gone?' she demanded, once a glance around the room confirmed he wasn't with me.

'I told him he'd have to go to the park without you,' I said levelly. 'I need to speak with you about something and it's not something that can wait. I told him you'd give him a call later.'

For all her self-proclaimed maturity, Elise did a very good exasperated fourteen-year-old eye-roll. '*What*?' she said. 'Why? What d'you need to speak to me about that's, like, *so* urgent? Can't it wait?' She glanced back towards the hall as if assessing the viability of simply turning tail and going after him anyway. But then, seeing me shake my head, seemed to think better of it. 'Okay, so *what*, then?' she finished, irritably tossing her hair back.

'Something quite serious,' I said, gesturing towards the dining table. 'Let's sit down, shall we?'

I had her full attention now. Well, at least, as she pulled out a chair to sit on, she looked as if she was taking things a little more seriously. Did she have some inkling about what I was going to tell her? I studied her expression carefully as we both sat down at the table. On opposite sides, as if at a domestic high noon.

'So,' I said, 'I've been having a conversation on Facebook. With someone called ...' I told her the woman's name.

No flicker of recognition. 'And?' she said. 'Is that something to do with me?'

'And she told me you'd been speaking to her husband on Messenger.' I gave Elise a short rundown of the gist

134

of the messages we'd exchanged. And as I spoke I watched her expression change from one of slight anxiety, through confusion, then on to something I could only describe as mild boredom – boredom! – once the penny, I assumed, finally dropped.

'So, first of all,' I finished, 'is this all true? And secondly, if it is true, I want to know why you did it. Is this man known to you?'

'Known to me?'

'Yes. Is he someone you know, Elise? Someone you've come into contact with before? Someone known to one of your parents? Someone from your past, perhaps?'

What I really wanted to ask, of course, was about the photographs in her biscuit tin of memories. Whether there might be any connection with this man and her earlier childhood. But I held back. I mustn't lead her. And it turned out to be a moot point anyway.

'*What*?' she said again. 'No, of *course* not! I've never even met him! Well, as in not *actually* met him.'

'So he's a complete stranger.'

'Yes, I *said*.'

'So what on *earth* inspired you to get in touch with him and send him all those images? What were you *thinking*, Elise?'

'*D'oh*. That he needed outing?'

'*Outing*? Elise, you're going to have to enlighten me here. What on earth are you talking about?'

'As in being exposed for what he is,' she explained. 'What else would I mean?'

'So, let me get this straight. You make contact with this man and send him explicit pictures of yourself, then, when he responds, you lead him on for a bit, sending messages and more pictures, then at some point you screenshot it all and sent it to his wife, yes?'

'Exactly.' She sat back, sounding pleased with herself. Well, at least momentarily. Till the moment she clocked the expression on *my* face. She sat forward again then. 'Okay, Casey. Look, I don't expect you to understand, but actually I was doing that woman a massive favour.'

This I had to hear. 'You're right, Elise,' I said. 'I definitely *don't* understand. How on earth do you work out that you've done her a favour? That poor woman has a child, and now her marriage and family are in tatters. So, the question is why? Why would you do that? What was going through your mind to make you think that was a good thing to do?'

Elise looked at me in much the same way as a teacher might to a child who was struggling with the same word over and over again. 'I don't know why you don't get it, Casey, but it's like this. I'm like one of those paedophile hunters you hear about all the time. You know the ones: they set up a fake profile on social media, as if they are a fourteen-year-old girl or whatever, in the hope that some pervert will make contact and want to meet them. They then go through with it, as if it's real, and when the pervert shows up, they report them to the police and expose them all over Facebook and stuff. I'm just doing the same thing, except I don't actually go meet them, and I *am* actually fourteen. It's really quite simple. These men deserve it. They are freaks!'

'*These* men? Elise, you just told me these men are complete strangers! How can you possibly decide they are "freaks", as you put it?'

Again that look, as if I was being really stupid. 'Because when I send them pictures they're, like, all over it, that's why. If they don't then they're not.' She shrugged. 'Simple.'

As I stared at her, I could feel my jaw dropping so far that I wouldn't have been surprised to hear my chin clunk onto the table. This girl genuinely believed she was providing some kind of valuable service to unsuspecting women, and here she was justifying destroying a family.

'So this isn't a one-off, then? You've been doing it with other men?'

Elise shook her head now. 'No,' she said. 'I just joined.'

'Joined?'

'The group.'

'What group?'

'The group on Facebook I joined.'

'You mean there's a whole group of you doing this? Hunting down likely candidates to send explicit photos to? To –' I was struggling to find the word to use. Entrapment? This was exactly that, wasn't it? 'To tempt to take the bait?' I continued.

'Oh, I think there's lots of them, actually. Look,' she continued, leaning further in, clearly keen to explain the mission now, 'These men need exposing. I know we're the ones who make contact, and yes, maybe some would say that's wrong, but –'

'How, though? How do you do that?'

'You just look out for them. You know, friends of friends of friends. The ones who like your profile picture, or comment on a picture you've been tagged in or something, or who send you friend requests, or make some sort of comment on a post by someone whose friend request you accepted, or –'

'Okay, I get the gist of that okay, but then what? You just send them a picture of yourself in your underwear?'

'No, of course not. You chat to them first, for a bit, and –' She shrugged. 'Like, just see what happens.'

She sounded chillingly as if she'd been schooled in all this. 'But it's only been this one man?'

'Yes, I told you. He was just a random guy who I picked when I was bored one night, and he seemed like the type, so I thought I'd test him out to prove my theory that all men are perverts.'

'And that's your theory, is it? That's why you joined this group?'

Elise shrugged again. 'Well, I was proved right first time, wasn't I? I mean, he could have rejected my messages, could have ignored them, he could have told me he was happily married and didn't want to get involved, but he didn't, did he? He wanted to play. I don't care what you say, Casey, his wife deserved to know.'

'And all this because you were *bored*?' I tried not to splutter it.

'Yeah, but not just that. I told you, these men have it coming to them.'

'Elise, a woman and her child are now in meltdown. Does that not mean anything to you? Okay, the man shouldn't have engaged with you, but it's you who started it all off. You should never have done something so stupid in the first place. It's –' I was groping for the right word again. 'It's … horrendous!'

'Oh my God, so you're saying you feel *sorry* for him, Casey? You think all the blame lies with me? That's just great. No wonder these paedos get away with it for so long.'

I shook my head, feeling both astounded and appalled. Feeling it would have been so much more manageable, so much more credible, if there had been some sort of connection with this man. As it was, she was as good as admitting she was a self-appointed vigilante, still adamant she was simply providing a service to 'out' these potential 'cheaters', and she couldn't see that by initiating the whole thing, *she* had made it happen. But where to start in trying to change her thinking? I was feeling increasingly at sea with this girl.

'Elise, I'm blaming you only for starting it off,' I pointed out. 'Yes, the man was definitely in the wrong too, but he might have gone his whole life *not* doing anything like this had you not tried to lure him in. Can't you see that?'

'He *might* have,' she said, 'but we would never know that, would we? If he were a real good guy, he would never have been tempted, so I'm sorry, but I still think I'm in the right here.'

I stood up. This was getting us nowhere. 'I'm sorry, love. You must understand that you did wrong. And it needs to stop. I don't want to ever hear that you've done this again, do you hear me, Elise? It has to stop. *Now*.'

'Fine,' she said, 'but if it's not me it will be some other girl. I told you, it's not just me tracking down these perverts and exposing them. There are *loads* of groups that find these pervs and expose them, but yes. *Fine*. I'll stop, then. Now can I go to my room, please? I need to phone Josh and fix up where to meet him.'

Just like that. Shrugged off and forgotten. I almost felt as if I'd been dismissed. I duly excused her, however. 'Though don't make any plans to go out tonight,' I added. 'I'm doing tea in half an hour and after that I'd like us all to do something as a family. I was thinking maybe a board game or a movie.'

'Fine!' she said again as she left the room. 'But I probably won't have time to join you with games or whatever, because I've got loads of homework to do and need to study for a biology test.'

I shook my head as I watched her go then went to rummage in the fridge for something to cook. *And while she's studying for biology*, I thought, *I think I need to catch up on a bit of psychology!* I was completely bemused by her way of thinking, not to mention feeling aghast that this seemed not to be just some idea she'd invented, but part of an organised online campaign she'd found her way to. And one of many engaged in the same dangerous practices, by the sound of things. A thought popped into my head, then. *What is the world coming to?* The rate of change in the world since the internet had been invented was so fast that I wasn't just struggling to keep up – I was completely losing track of the multiple ways it was spiralling into new and scary territory. And that wasn't just me being an old fuddy-duddy either. Social media increasingly seemed to be rewriting the rules about how humans interacted with one another. No, more than that – throwing the rules out of the window and inventing completely new ones. And none of us yet knew what the implications of such a massive social change were going to be – only that there *would* almost certainly be implications. There already were; the statistics about young girls and body-image and deteriorating mental health were already particularly chilling.

And now this, I thought, as I continued to hunt in the fridge. Teenage girls setting up as vigilantes? I really couldn't believe that such things went on in the world. How did they even think up these things? It made me feel sick to the stomach, if I was being honest.

Having decided on pork chops, I left them on the side alongside some potatoes and vegetables, then I took my mobile phone out to the garden. I needed to phone Christine Bolton while this was all still fresh in my mind.

'Bloody hell, Casey!' she said after I'd given her the lowdown. 'That poor woman. That poor *child*! It almost beggars belief.'

Christine felt exactly the same as I did – dismayed that such activities were apparently widespread on the internet and as concerned about the potential implications. She also agreed that though the man had acted stupidly and recklessly, he was likely far from the first and unlikely to be the last – probably more likely he'd be one in a pretty lengthy line as long as there were girls like Elise stalking the internet, out to tempt them.

'But it's what's driving it that concerns me the most,' I told Christine. 'This apparent conviction that all men are monsters. Or would be, given half a chance. It's so depressing. I just wish I could find a way into her psyche. Some little chink that would allow me to see the bigger picture.'

'Well, there's at least one positive I can report,' Christine answered. 'I've found out today that her new social worker has been assigned. Holly Davies. I don't know her personally. She's new to the area, and quite new to the job. But she comes with great references, and has been fully genned up on all things Elise. And maybe – since she *is* new – she'll be full of energy and enthusiasm.' She chuckled. 'Well, for a while yet, at any rate.'

'How old is she?'

'Early thirties. And she's come from a teaching background. Secondary. So that's a plus – she'll be well used to the peccadillos of teenage girls, and Elise won't take one look at her and think she's ancient. Oh, and I'm definitely getting help from CAMHS. This latest incident only endorses our case for an intervention.'

'But I thought you said she wouldn't engage with them?'

'Engage or not, we still need Elise to be in their system,' Christine said. 'I have a feeling that with this girl we will need to dot all the 'i's and cross all the 't's, so even if they see her and she doesn't speak a word, they can keep trying and at least we've covered that base. That way, at least nobody can say we didn't do it all by the book.' I heard her sigh now. 'Other than that, I'm not sure what else to do. Let's just hope that new blood, in the shape of Holly, will help. Oh, and I filled her in about those photos you saw – and maybe Elise will open up to her as she's nearer her own age. Anyway, are *you* okay? You did the right thing, by the way, telling that woman only what you did, but do you need anything else? You only have to ask if you need a couple of nights' break, some respite or whatever?'

'No, I'm fine,' I said, 'though thanks for the offer. I think you're right about trying again with CAMHS – you never know, she might be willing to give it a go this time. For my part, I'll continue to try to get her to open up as well, and although I can't take her phone off her, I'll keep reminding her not to be so silly in the future.'

As if 'silly' even remotely described the dangerous game she'd been playing. In the end I was glad that Elise decided to take herself up to her room after tea as it gave me the chance to catch Mike up on my horrendous day, but I felt very sorry for him as the implications began to sink in.

'What's that film?' he mused. 'You know, the sci-fi one. With Tom Cruise. *Minority Report* – that's the one. Where they can intervene and stop crimes before they even happen because those pre-cogs can predict when they're going to take place. Except *she* can't. This is just another example of her mad vendettas. She's seriously disturbed, love. And dangerous. I mean, she can actually destroy lives. A word, an accusation, an innocent remark twisted. Jesus! If I felt like I was walking on eggshells around her before, now I feel I dare not be in the same bloody room as her. Question is, what exactly are we going to do?'

I shook my head, unable to reassure him I had a plan. Because, right now, that was a question I had no answer to.

Chapter 14

Because Elise believed she had done nothing wrong, and wouldn't even consider the alternative, life continued pretty much as normal. After an uneventful weekend came an equally uneventful week; she got up on time every day for school, was meticulous about keeping her room clean and doing chores, was polite to a fault and always did her homework before going off out anywhere with friends. In fact, on paper, she was the poster child for a happy teenager in care and I caught myself more than once wondering exactly what my role was beyond providing the proverbial roof over her head. But I couldn't unsee the photos I had found in her tin, and I couldn't forget the long list of dramas she'd been involved in, most of them, no question, having been instigated *by* her. And though I'd had no further contact from the woman whose husband she'd sent the explicit pictures and messages to, the very fact of what she'd been up to, even if she didn't do it again, meant she had some serious psychological issues. And if they weren't addressed how long would it be until she got herself into equally serious trouble? Trouble was, though, that it would be *me* who would have to upset the apple cart and coax her to visit places in her head which she clearly didn't want to revisit.

Still at least I had a new ally, in the form of her new social worker, Holly Davies, who had emailed to introduce herself a couple of days after I'd spoken to Christine and who'd suggested she pay a visit at the end of that week, both for us to get acquainted and, once Elise was back from school, to have a short informal meeting with her as well.

I'd decided not to tell Elise that Holly was coming, only that she needed to come straight home from school that day – I was worried that if she knew someone from 'the social' was coming over she might 'accidentally' forget or make up some excuse. Holly, who had arrived half an hour before Elise was due home, agreed with my strategy because she liked to 'go in cold', getting a more accurate picture of what a child was really like as opposed to the version they might present if they had time to get their guard up.

I liked Holly immediately; she had a natural warmth about her, and though she was young, as Christine had said, she seemed full of ambition, having made the switch from teaching and all that endless marking, but mostly the 'tyranny of the school bell'.

'You'll still have plenty of paperwork to wade through,' I felt the need to point out, 'but if you want something that's never the same two days running I reckon you've definitely chosen the right career. Well, as long as you're flexible about the definition of the word "day", that is …'

Holly assured me that the on-calls, particularly the nights, were actually one of her favourite parts of the job. 'I like the adrenaline rush,' she admitted, 'never knowing what you're going to be faced with.' And though I suspected down the line she might get a little worn down on that front (there are only so many small-hours snatches of abused children that you could stomach without beginning to feel disheartened and world-weary), I got what she meant and really admired her candour. I was glad to have her on board.

Elise was rather less enthusiastic. 'What? *Why?*' she asked when she arrived home and I explained who Holly, sitting in the living room, was. 'Why do I need another flipping social worker when I'm doing fine and settled in here?'

I held a hand out for the blazer she was shrugging from her shoulders. She was as aware as I was that the 'flipping social worker' in question was only metres away, beyond the open door. 'Elise, don't be rude,' I chided, as Holly turned around and waved. 'Of course you still have a social worker, and you will have until either you're eighteen or leave care. It's the way things are, and you already know that. So how about you head in and say hello, while I go and put the kettle on?'

As I'd already established when the two of us had sat and discussed Elise's file, Holly had definitely done her homework. And I don't know if it was research or intuition or a combination of both, but when I returned with tea and coffee, Elise already seemed a different girl, having forgotten her mood about being visited by a social worker, and was now in full chatty, giggly, charm-offensive mode.

In return, Holly seemed genuinely charmed by her. Well, I say 'genuinely', but I suspect it was a little more complicated than that. I knew Holly knew how superficial Elise could be because we'd already discussed it, and I had a hunch she was 'playing' her right back. When they got quickly onto the serious business about the Facebook fiasco, she was straight away, and very firmly, on Team Elise.

'Oh, absolutely,' she agreed, after Elise expounded her philosophy about the evil nature of men in general. 'I can see how you thought you'd be doing this lady a favour. I can *absolutely* get how you felt. The way that man behaved was nothing short of disgraceful.'

'Exactly what I said!' Elise spluttered, looking pointedly at me as I poured Holly a mug of tea. 'But *some* people just don't understand that.'

At which point I would have normally jumped in and said my piece, but Holly was already one step ahead of me. 'Having said *that*,' she went on, 'you're on complicated ground. If you think about it, that silly, *silly* man might never have done anything like that if nobody had ever messaged him and offered him pictures.' She then held up her hand to stop Elise interrupting. 'I know, I know – he still had no right, he really didn't. But you know, some men, and women actually, are just so easily led on by things like this. Honestly, Elise, they really aren't worth bothering with and they are *definitely* not worth you getting into trouble with the police over.'

'Getting into trouble with the *police*?' Elise asked, suddenly looking worried. 'How would *I* get into trouble with the police? I was *helping* them!'

'Well, I think they call it enticement, and then, of course, there's the more serious charge of sharing explicit material, over which the police might well have been involved. Because that poor wife could have reported you to them for sharing explicit photos online – and we can't forget that the man could have actually shared your photos all over the internet by now, especially if he was that angry at what happened.'

'Jesus!' Elise said, her sculpted eyebrows shooting up. 'Really? He could do that? And *I'd* be the one in trouble?'

'Sadly, yes. At least in theory. Which is why we all need to be hyper-careful about the sort of thing we upload to the internet. And as we both know, you never *really* know who you're dealing with, do you? It's just so easy to create an avatar and stay anonymous.' Holly smiled then, and placed a matey, girls-in-solidarity hand briefly on Elise's arm. 'Don't worry. To be honest, if I were him, I'd just want the whole thing to go away. Anyway, you'll just have to keep your fingers crossed, won't you? And obviously not upload those sorts of images again, however strongly you feel it's for the right reasons.'

Elise was busy nodding now. 'God, no. I won't!' And I looked on, bemused at the difference in response compared to the conversation she'd had with me. But I also realised the key difference in Holly's approach; instead of challenging Elise's skewed world view, that all men were potential rapists, she'd focused on the potential for Elise getting into trouble herself, and that had clearly done the trick.

Which was a big positive. Clearly this social worker knew what she was doing. I had a feeling that Holly Davies and I were going to get along just fine and, so far, that she and Elise would as well. Well, at least I did till the subject of a CAMHS (child and adolescent mental health services) appointment came up, to which Elise shook her head firmly. On this, she really did seem immovable.

'I'm sorry, Holly. I know it's not your fault. I know your manager or whoever has told you to ask me, but I won't talk to them so it's completely pointless making me go. All they want me to do is talk about my past and I'm not prepared to do that with a stranger. I'm just not. Would *you* want to do that? Just sit there with a complete randomer and tell them stuff that's private? And what for, exactly?' she went on. 'What's the point of it? That's all in the past and what good would it do to bring it all up again?'

Holly nodded sympathetically. 'I hear you, Elise. And I totally take your point – and I also respect where you're coming from. But these services are offered not to make things worse for you – they're to *help* you. To help you revisit things that have happened to you, things that might have upset or traumatised you, things that might impact on how you feel now, even if you've tucked them away in your subconscious, out of reach. And to –'

'I feel *fine*. That's the whole point. I'm not a nut job, so why does everyone keep wanting me to go back over all that stuff? Specially with a stranger. It'll just make me upset all over again.'

'Initially, perhaps,' Holly started. 'But the whole point of counselling is that it gives you the opportunity to deal with aspects of your past that are giving you emotional issues in the present, and which –'

'But I don't *have* any "emotional issues", as you call them.' She put the words in finger quote marks. 'I'm not some head case who needs fixing. I'm fine as I *am*. I just want people to stop going on and on at me all the time about stuff that doesn't matter anymore.'

I could sense the growing frustration in Elise's voice, so, anxious that we didn't undo the good work already done, decided to step in.

'You don't have to, love. Not right now. Not if you don't want to. Loads of people – and this is true of lots of kids we've looked after too – find counselling a great way to help manage their demons, and work through things that are hard to talk about, but if it's not for you, it's not for you.' I glanced at Holly. 'I think we both just want you to know that we are here for you. In your corner. That there is help for you if you want it. But if you don't, then so be it … And right now,' I glanced at my watch, 'I think I'd better get the tea on. Look at the time! I'm going to have two starving men arriving home within the hour and I've not even made a start.'

'Quite,' Holly agreed, pulling her jacket from the back of the dining chair. 'Though it'll be a take-away for me. Friday night equals curry night. No exceptions! Anyway, it was lovely meeting you, Elise. And there's a thought. Do you like Indian food? Perhaps next time I come we could pop out for a curry together? Or some-thing else if you'd rather? After school one day, maybe? It will be good to get to know each other a little better, won't it?'

Elise looked a little shocked. 'Go out together?'

Holly nodded. 'Yes, of course.'

'What, like just the two of us?'

'Just the two of us.' She grinned. 'Don't look so surprised. That's what I'm here for. I mean, obviously, my job is to be there for you professionally, but, you know, I'd like to think we can become friends as well. If you'd like that?'

'Well, yeah, course,' Elise said, shrugging. 'Yeah, cool. If you want. That'll be fine.'

But beyond that shrug, for all that Elise talked about her many, many friends, I sensed that *this* offer of friendship, both unsolicited and unexpected, had come as quite a shock. And in a good way.

I spent a few restless hours that night wondering just how *I* was going to find a way into Elise. For all her talk of not being a 'head case' or a 'nut job', as she'd put it (and the very fact that she used such terms for anyone with mental health issues spoke volumes in itself), actions invariably spoke louder than words, and her case file contained more than enough evidence to suggest otherwise.

But how to 'unlock' her? I knew that I could actually just ride out this time with her and have an easy life. In theory, if nothing changed, for the next four years. I knew that, all other things being equal, and with no further dramas, that would probably suit the girl perfectly. She worked hard to show me only the near-perfect, sunny side of her, and would presumably do that with Holly too. And the truth was that what you didn't know about couldn't hurt you. So, whatever she did outside of home, if I didn't hear about it, or feel its impact, then it wouldn't even affect me.

But, of course, that's not what fostering is all about. My heart and gut – always the most reliable of indicators – were both telling me that in order to do my job right I *would* have to upset the apple cart. I would have to push Elise to talk, and risk making waves

– potentially big ones – in the calm waters of our *Stepford Wives*-like existence. If I didn't, I wouldn't be helping her to move forward with her life in an emotionally healthy way. It was just a question of how to tease her out of her shell.

The answer came, in the end, rather unexpectedly. It was the following Wednesday night and we'd not long waved Tyler and Naomi off. They were going to drive to York that evening for an overnight stay, Tyler having a second interview with a leisure centre there the following morning. 'Though they're just crossing "i"s and "t"s,' Ty had reassured me. 'Just want to show me round the place, meet the team and everything.' And I didn't doubt it. He'd already had two online interviews on something called 'Teams', and the move was now apparently planned for a couple of weeks hence, him apparently having already given his notice.

I couldn't feel sad for them. Far from it. Now I'd got my head around the idea I was really quite excited. Their own excitement was infectious, of course, but it wasn't just that. I was already imagining all the visits we'd be making and thinking how nice it would be to help them with the move. 'And having a proper clear-out,' Mike had also pointed out. 'There must be tons of old junk we can offload on them …'

I was in a determinedly buoyant mood after tea that evening, and had even ventured up into the loft to go through some bits and bobs for them while Mike caught up with one of his police procedurals on TV. I was just backing down the loft ladder with an armful of bedding when I became aware that Elise was standing in Ty's bedroom doorway.

'You okay, love?' I asked her, since she seemed to want to speak to me. She'd gone up to her room after tea to do some schoolwork and chat to mates online (well, hopefully), but she was now gazing into Ty's room, looking thoughtful.

'Yeah … I was just thinking. When Tyler leaves can I move into this room? It's so much bigger than mine, and it's got that huge wardrobe.'

I put the pile of bedding down and brushed my fringe off my damp forehead. It had been a hot couple of days and the loft space was like a sauna. 'You don't let the grass grow, do you?' I said. 'He hasn't even moved out yet!'

'I know, but, you know, when he does, like I said.'

I didn't need to think about it, even for a second. I shook my head. 'No, love, I'm sorry, but that's his room.'

'I know, but it won't be once he's moved out, so I thought –'

'And still has all his stuff in it. Plus, they'll still be wanting to come back for weekends, won't they? Anyway, you've already got a perfectly nice room. So no, love. Sorry.'

'But we can move his stuff into my room and he can sleep there when he comes back. It's not like he's going to mind, is it?' She rolled her eyes. 'It's just a *room*.'

I didn't know who wasn't quite reading the other right – perhaps we both weren't – but at that I felt my whole body stiffen. 'It's not just a room, love. It's my *son's* room. And I'd quite like it to remain so, at least for the time being, so he and Naomi have it here for them to use when they come and stay.'

I was already beginning to feel cross with myself. Why on earth was I explaining myself to this fourteen-year-old? But still she pressed on. 'I know, I get that, but I'm here all the time. Because I *live* here. And it's much bigger –'

'Elise, your room is hardly small.'

'And it has a bigger bed, and the bay window, and if I go in there I'll have room for an actual desk to do my *schoolwork*.'

Was it the pointed way she'd said 'schoolwork' that did it? Or just my heightened emotional state? In either event, I had to consciously stop myself from snapping at her – things I had no business even thinking, let alone saying, like who did she think she was dictating her sleeping arrangements and telling me I was being unreasonable in not immediately complying with her requests? Instead, as levelly as I could, I said, 'It's not up for debate, Elise.'

And that was when she really blew the lid off. 'I don't know why it's such an *issue*,' she said. 'And it's not like it's unfair. Not when you think about it. What's the difference, after all? I mean, *he* was your foster kid and now *I* am your foster kid, so why is my going in there such a big deal?'

I Just Want to be Loved

To which my instinctive answer was that Tyler wasn't 'just' my foster kid, he was my son, and she knew that. And even if he had 'just' been my foster kid – a term I didn't like one bit – that was beside the point. My house. My bedrooms. My decision on who slept where. No way her prerogative to demand that she move across the landing, or even start to challenge me when I'd already told her she couldn't. Who the hell did she think she was?

But somehow I managed not to say any of that. Mostly because another thought came along immediately after that lot. That this was, in fact – or had become – a challenge of a different kind. To test my mettle. To see if she could bend my will by suggesting there was a stark difference between Tyler's and her place in my affections. She might not have realised that consciously, but to me it was screamingly obvious. They were *not* comparable. He was a beloved son and she was exactly what she'd striven to be since she'd come to us – a virtual stranger for whom, at her repeated request, we did little more than just provide bed and board.

Perhaps her intention when asking if she could move rooms had not been that initially. Perhaps she really had just fancied moving to the bigger, sunnier room. But now it was – I could read that in the challenge in her eyes. *Spell it out*, they seemed to say. *Remind me how little I matter. Reinforce my belief that I'm unloved and on my own in the world.*

It was blindingly clear, though, that this was not a battle to be won. No way was Elise having Tyler's bedroom – not now, and not in the foreseeable future – but no way was I going to let her use my refusal as a stick to beat me with. So, I regrouped and chose my words carefully.

'How do you think Tyler would feel,' I asked her, 'to be turfed out of his room before the bed's even cold? It doesn't matter that he's off to begin his life with Naomi, and I'm sure his fervent hope is that it'll all work out brilliantly and that this is the start of a lifelong journey together – believe me, it's mine too – but to turf him out of his room, to rip down his posters and throw his childhood possessions into a box at the very first opportunity isn't just unseemly, it's not right. In time, if all goes well, he'll sort his own stuff out, bit by bit, and one day, yes, you are right, this room will no longer be his bedroom. But that time isn't now. This is a big life transition for him, another one, and this room,' I cast my arm around, 'is a safety net, a security blanket, an expression of love and family. Does that go some way to explaining how it *is* actually a big deal?'

There was a moment of silence, our gazes locked across the landing. 'Fine!' she said eventually. 'Lucky *him*!' Then she went back into her room and slammed the door with enough force to make the floor shake.

I walked slowly down the stairs, thinking hard about what had just happened, and was then filled with an entirely unexpected emotion.

'Something going down up there?' Mike asked, gesturing upwards, when I popped my head round the living-room door.

I checked the time. I'd make a coffee and give it fifteen or twenty minutes. 'You know what?' I said. 'I do believe we might be about to make some progress.'

Chapter 15

Elise was in bed when I knocked and went into her room. Lying on her side in the semi-dark, facing the wall, the glow from her phone screen illuminating half her face.

'What?' she asked sullenly when she heard me come in, but what she didn't do was tell me I should have waited until she answered, or ask me to leave, or anything at all, in fact. She just carried on scrolling.

Taking that as a positive, I crossed the room and sat down at the end of the bed. 'You're right, you know,' I began, 'about Tyler being lucky. We're incredibly lucky, too, to have him, but he has been very lucky, to have arrived, at the right time, at the right place, with the right family. It's not always the case. Some children come here and then leave and move on to other families. Fostering isn't the same as adoption, as you know. And some head home, or to other family members. But you got me thinking and I realised you

know very little about him – after all, why would you?
– and it occurred to me that you actually have a lot in
common. As in the sort of childhood traumas you've
both suffered.' I paused there, but Elise remained
exactly as she was, scrolling through images in some
social media feed or other. Which I took to be a good
sign. So I carried on.

'Tyler's mum was a heroin addict and she died of an
overdose when he was three. He was found by a neighbour naked and sitting crying by his mother's body.
He'd been there for some time and was by then in quite
a state. So, his dad had to step up, and he did, at least in
theory. He'd had no contact with his ex or his son up to
that point, and was by then with a new partner, and
she'd only recently given birth to their baby. And she
didn't really want anything to do with Tyler. With *any*
of it. I mean, she tried, of course she did, but her heart
wasn't in it. She had her own son and she really didn't
want to have to also look after a traumatised three-year-
old too. And from what I've heard about your
stepmother … well, I'm sure that scenario will be familiar to you …'

I paused again, more to draw breath than anything;
in all my years of fostering, the memory of Tyler's stepmother still burned so ferociously bright. It wasn't for
me to judge, much less condemn, but it was still so hard
to fathom how anyone, particularly someone who was a
mother herself, could be as unremitting cruel to an
innocent child as she had been to Tyler. 'Anyway, that's

how it started,' I finished, 'and why Ty eventually ended up in care.'

I sensed movement. 'So, what happened?' she said, still on her side, facing away from me. 'Did he run away or something?'

I shook my head. 'No. When he was eleven, he ended up in a police station – that was where I first saw him – having stabbed her with a carving knife. She said deliberately, and pressed charges and completely disowned him; he said accidentally, after a row during which he had pulled it from the cutlery drawer and threatened to kill her with it. He said he never would have. It was just an empty threat. But she was injured while she was trying to get it off him.'

Now she turned to face me, looking up at me from over her shoulder. 'And you believed him?'

'Once I had the facts, knew the bigger picture, yes I did. Absolutely. But I also understood that he'd been in so much pain, and for so long, that even if it *had* been true, I would have fostered him anyway. He had nowhere to go and not a soul alive who truly loved him. That kind of hurt doesn't easily go away. Being rejected like that – by both the stepmother who didn't want him and the father who didn't either ... well, can you imagine how that felt at age eleven? I think you can.'

Her response was immediate. 'My dad loved me. It was *her*.'

'Your mum?'

Elise shook her head. 'No, my *step*mum. If he hadn't got with *her* …' She lapsed into silence again.

I waited for a second, watched her slip her phone under her pillow. Then risked it. 'Then you wouldn't have been sent back to your mum?'

'*Exactly.*' Elise rolled onto her back now, then shuffled up so she was half-sitting now, against the pillows. 'I mean, who would even *do* something like that anyway?'

I was confused now. 'You mean your stepmum?'

'No, my *real* mum. What kind of mother would just leave her only child? It would have actually been *better* if she'd been a druggie, and then died of an overdose. At least that would have been something that wasn't her *fault*, wouldn't it? Abandoning me wouldn't have been her *decision*.'

Understanding her train of thought now – that leap from stepmum to real mum, and *her* rejection of Elise – I felt on tenterhooks now, sensing how easily this could slip away from me. This was clearly something she had thought about a lot. Something she'd gone over in her head time and time again, probably. Asking the same question – how could her mother have just walked away and abandoned her in the first place?

The answer would no doubt be complex – perhaps too complex for her young mind to deal with, the pain too raw to allow for understanding, the reality that followed too grim and all-consuming for her to see her mum's actions through a more forgiving light – one tempered by accepting that not all mums are perfect, and some end up not fit to be mothers at all, and sometimes through no fault of their own.

Up to now I knew little about Elise's birth mother, but it seemed I was about to find out. 'You know,' she said, suddenly animated, intense, 'when my dad tracked her down and made her take me back, she'd already had another kid! Can you believe that? Just left me and Dad and gone off and had another one. And you know the worst bit? I didn't care! I was just so happy to escape that evil bitch! I couldn't wait to go and live with her. I was finally going to escape from that witch of a step-mother who hated me, and go and be with my real mum. I was actually *pleased*!' She shook her head, the bitterness in her voice all too painfully evident. 'I mean, how stupid can you be?'

'Not stupid. You were just a child, Elise.'

'Yes stupid. I thought once I was there she'd be *pleased* to have me back. And she was, too. To be her baby-minder, that's why!'

'That's so sad. I'm so sorry to hear what you went through.'

'Oh, it gets worse, believe me.' She laughed mirth-lessly. 'It was like I'd been promised a fairy tale and had actually just been thrown into a snake pit!'

She was on a roll now, and I listened in silence, my heart breaking for her, as she so eloquently described how she'd been left at such a young age to look after her two-year-old half-sister, Saffy, while her mum enter-tained male 'friends' behind locked doors. How she often got up to find that her mother hadn't come home all night and how she would then have to wash, dress and feed the little one all by herself, often with no idea of when her mother might be home. Or, sometimes, who she might come home *with*. And – most heartbreaking of all, this – she did all of this because she wanted to be helpful. She thought if she could be useful it would make her mum love her. Then the shocking reality, as the scales fell from her eyes and it gradually dawned on her what her mother did to earn money; how she would bring men home at all hours and insist that Elise put on a school uniform, wear make-up and tie bows in her hair.

I thought of the photos I'd seen and I shuddered.

'I had three school uniforms and no bloody school,' she went on. 'And all so dirty old men could get their kicks from looking at me, taking photos and making videos.'

The air felt thick with her revulsion. 'How long were you with your mum, Elise?'

'Till I couldn't stand it any longer. I don't know. About two years. I hated leaving my little sister *so* much but …' She paused, screwed a bit of duvet up in clenched fists. 'It was getting worse. With the "uncles". That's what she called the regulars. Our "uncles".'

'So, you ran away.'

Elise nodded. 'All the way to my nan's. My dad's mum. I couldn't go back to Dad's, not with that witch there. And Nan wasn't speaking to him then anyway, because of him throwing me out.'

'So, your nan took you in.'

She nodded again, unshed tears shining in her eyes now, and seemed to be struggling to hold herself together, some new memory perhaps surfacing, some other scar sloughing off. She couldn't speak but I could also see just how hard she was trying not to cry. This was clearly enough for her. More than enough.

I reached an arm out and covered her hands with one of my own. 'It's okay to cry, love,' I said softly. But still she wrestled with herself and tried to rein in the sob that was clearly becoming too powerful to contain. She snatched her hands away then and covered her face with them, and as her shoulders began to shudder I couldn't help noticing the contrast between this distressed child and the perfectly manicured nails that were such a part of the persona she showed to the world.

I watched and waited, unsure whether to speak or try to comfort her, but instinct told me to stay where I was. She had opened the door on some pretty painful memories and I wasn't sure she was ready or even able to go further, as her defence against pain was to keep the past locked away, and exposing her vulnerability, to me or anyone, was probably distressing her almost as much. So, I eventually stood up. 'Shall I make you a warm drink, love?' I asked her. 'Or get some squash?'

She shook her head and sniffed, her hands still covering her face. 'I'm okay,' she said. 'Sorry ...' She sniffed again. 'I'm so sorry ...'

'Elise, sweetheart,' I reassured her, 'you have absolutely nothing to be sorry for.' Which only produced a fresh bout of shudders.

'I'm okay,' she said again. 'I just can't … don't … I just want to go to sleep now.'

'Of course,' I said, nodding, as her hands finally lowered. 'And remember, I'm here if you need me.'

And then I left her, blowing her nose with a handful of tissues from her box, and went downstairs to fire up my laptop – keen to get everything down while it was fresh in my mind. *Finally*, I thought. At last a tiny window through which a hint of the real child could be seen – the first steps on the road to help her healing. I also needed to get it sent off to Christine via email. Because Elise's grim disclosures didn't just corroborate the evidence I'd seen in those photographs. They also hinted towards something equally disturbing – and urgent. The potential danger Elise's half-sister might be in too.

Chapter 16

The next morning, I expected Elise to be a little withdrawn, given the serious nature of what we had talked about. Perhaps reticent, even, troubled that she'd let her guard slip. She acted, however, as if nothing had happened, much less been said, and, after replying to my, 'You okay, love?' with a resounding, 'Yes, fine!', headed off to school without, seemingly, a care in the world. The mask, then, was firmly back in place.

I had no such tricks up my sleeve to help me glide through the day, though I couldn't help but marvel at the ability of the human brain. Just how many kids had passed through our hands now who could do such effective disappearing acts with their emotions? Too many. The miserable truth was that the origin of such desperate measures was almost always a pretty desperate situation.

I still had no idea of the extent of the abuse Elise had suffered, though the nature of it seemed pretty unequivocal. It also made perfect sense that she knew all about the power of indecent images and that she'd used it in her nascent online mission to expose paedophiles. It was sickening to contemplate. I was surprised, then, when Christine called me an hour or so later, to hear her take on the email I'd sent her. Which was to wonder if we should automatically believe Elise. After all, she pointed out, it had been only a few short weeks ago that she had appeared in hysterics in our living room, accusing Jan Howard of all sorts.

'And it's not as if that was an isolated incident, is it?' she added. 'It's one in a very long line of blatant untruths.'

I took in what she said. Could she be right? Had I actually been played? Was this her way of getting CAMHS off her back? I couldn't quite believe it, though. The way the conversation had come about, the way she'd spoken and looked, and the way she'd cried – or, rather, tried so hard *not* to – all these told me that in this case she *was* being honest. Even Elise couldn't fake those emotions. 'And don't forget the photos,' I reminded Christine. 'What she's disclosed fits with them.'

'And we have a duty to act as if she's telling the truth anyway,' Christine conceded, just as we've done with all the poor souls she's already put through the ringer. So, we'll need to get an appointment with CAMHS as soon as possible, and hope she's prepared to make the same disclosures to them as well. And I agree, if this *is* true and not the girl crying wolf again about what could be an innocent, or innocent-of-a-crime-at-least, mother, then this half-sister could well be at risk. Not that it's simply a case of rocking up and asking questions. First, we'll need to find out where her mother *is*. As far as I know the last address we had on file was quite an old one, which she left without a forwarding address.'

'It can't be that hard, not these days,' I said.

'I think they tried *pretty* hard when she first came to our notice,' Christine reminded me, just stopping short of, quite rightly, ticking me off.

'How about the sister? That should help, shouldn't it? Saffy isn't a common name, is it? And what about the gran? Now she's out of hospital – and she might know something more, mightn't she?'

'She might. Anyway, leave all that side of things to me. You concentrate on Elise and the CAMHS appointment I'm going to get for her. There's little we can do without her co-operation on that front. And also her willingness to share those photos, don't forget.'

Which left me knowing that my next job would be to sit Elise down and spell it out to her that if we were going to help her, then she needed to dive back into the murky pool of her past, however painful that was going to be. Or not. Because in reality she *didn't* need to, did she? Yes, she'd opened up to me and told me things, but that could equally be the end of it. If she subsequently decided not to go there again, then it *would* be the end of it. And that was her choice, not mine.

But, as it turned out, it wasn't either me or Christine who facilitated the meeting with her mother. It was Elise herself.

Knowing there was no urgency about preparing Elise for a meeting with a CAMHS counsellor, as it would probably take a couple of weeks yet, I took her lead over the weekend and made no mention of anything to do with our conversation that night. And I would leave it that way till she herself volunteered anything further or an imminent appointment came through. We were preoccupied anyway with Ty and Naomi's impending move. Having secured both jobs and flat now, they were both working out notice and the date had been set for the Saturday three weeks hence. Being the kind of family we were, there was no way we'd do it by halves either. By the middle of the following week we'd arranged that a family deputation would be going up overnight, to see them both properly installed, and to take them out for dinner, so I was just about to call Christine to ask about a quick twenty-four-hour respite when her name popped up on my phone screen as an incoming call.

'Is Elise in school?' was her first question after we'd exchanged our hellos.

'Yes,' I said. 'Why?'

'Because I have just had the most bizarre conversation. With, would you believe, her *mother*. I mean, I was stunned. We've been trying to trace her for such a long time, and suddenly she pops up, bold as you like, saying she's been the one trying to track *us* down! And guess what? She is demanding to see her daughter.'

'*Seriously*?'

'Oh, yes indeed. And she's pretty emphatic about it, too. She said there is no court order banning this – which there isn't – and that we need to arrange something as soon as possible or she will be going to a solicitor about it.'

'Wow!' I said. 'Can she really do this? Demand to see her just like that? What about all the stuff that Elise disclosed the other night?'

'That's the thing, Casey. Doesn't it seem strange to you that Elise told you all of that last week, and then, only days later, I get the call from the very mother who numerous people have been trying to trace for months? Coincidence? I don't think so.'

'So, you think they've been in contact?'

'I think it's highly likely.'

'So, she didn't say they had?'

'No. I asked her that very question and the answer was no. She was pretty snippy about it too. And when I asked her why she wanted to see her, she was snippy about that too, telling me that I had no right to stop her or question her. And in answer to your question, she's right re: that first bit. Unless a judge had made a "no contact" order, which he hasn't, then she has a right to see Elise if it's what they both want. You're going to need to speak with the girl and ask her, obviously, and also try to get it out of her if they've been having virtual contact, because if that *is* the case, and they do want to see each other, then I definitely have reservations about the validity of what she told you. It could all be true of course, but still, knowing Elise as we do, we need to tread carefully here.'

Christine was right of course. This bolt out of the blue certainly changed things and threw up some questions, such as why now? And were mum and daughter in cahoots for some reason that I couldn't fathom at the moment? More than that, would an encounter put Elise at risk in some way? Without any certainty or complete trust in what Elise had already disclosed, then, yes, we would have to tread very carefully.

Which meant that a couple of hours later, I greeted Elise home from school with a slightly churning stomach, having turned everything over in my mind countless times in an attempt to work out what she and her mother might be up to. And more to the point, *why*?

Happily, I was at least partly reassured. As soon as I told Elise that her mum had been in touch and wanted to see her, her response was unequivocal and looked genuine. She groaned. But it definitely wasn't in shock.

'Oh God,' she said. '*Really*?'

I nodded. 'You don't sound as if this has come completely out of the blue, Elise. Have you been in contact with her?'

Elise's shoulders slumped. 'Yes, but only because of Saffy. I just kept thinking about her after talking to you – I just feel so bad that I left her there. I just thought if I could see her, maybe on FaceTime, just so I know she's okay … so I found my mum and messaged her.'

'On Facebook?'

She shook her head. 'No. Insta.'

'And this is the first time you've had contact with her since you went to your gran's?'

'Kind of.'

'Kind of?'

'I used to check her out a bit at first, after Nan took me in, just now and then …'

She looked abashed. And I realised that despite her upset when she'd told me about those 'uncles', running away from her mum and half-sister must still have been a difficult decision. This was her mum, after all, and she had been so young. Could I imagine any of mine running away at so young an age? No. But then mine hadn't spent their early lives in such emotional pain, or been abandoned by one parent then rejected by the other. She'd have been far from an ordinary ten-year-old, for sure.

'But then I stopped,' she said. 'I didn't want my nan finding out. And I didn't want her coming after me or anything.'

I was struck by her choice of words. Not 'trying to persuade her to come home', but 'coming after'. I might have been overthinking it, but in light of what I knew it sounded slightly menacing. 'Why d'you think she'd have done that?' I asked her.

She rolled her eyes a little. 'Because I was, like, her *slave*?'

I nodded. 'Okay, I see. But how did you manage to find her after all this time anyway? You know social services have been trying to trace her since you came into the care system?'

Now her eyes widened. 'Why would they *do* that?'

'Because she's your mum, love. It's part of their job to try and trace all a child's close relatives when they come into care.'

'God, they don't want to send me back there, do they? They can't make me, can they?'

'No, sweetie. Not unless you wanted to and they were satisfied about your safety and well-being. But in light of the things you've told me, I'm guessing that's *not* what you'd want. And you don't have to see her if you don't want to, either.'

'But what about Saffy? Can I see her?'

'Almost certainly, but only if she's with her mother. But Elise, love, I need to better understand what's going on here. How did you find her when nobody else could?'

'I just searched a few names I knew. It didn't take very long. She had this boyfriend whose surname I remembered she used to use. You know, for online and stuff.'

I didn't know. Well, I did. But I definitely didn't get it. The whole business of having online 'alter egos' still bemused me. Yes, clearly, if you were up to no good it made sense to create one, but it seemed no one felt the need to identify themselves anymore, not in the virtual

# # # # #

s# # # #

# # # # #

world, anyway. 'Well,' I said, 'now you've made contact, and she knows where you are – well, at least that social services know where you are. And now you've done that, is that what you think she wants now? For you to go back to her? Is that what you mean by her coming after you? Did she go round to your gran's and try to get you to go home before?'

'God, no. She wouldn't have gone near my nan. She would have *battered* her.'

'So, did you tell your nan any of what you told me last week?'

'God, no!' she said again. 'Tell my *nan* stuff like *that*? I just told her I didn't like my mum's boyfriend, and was sick of babysitting, and that I wanted to go back to school.'

It was hard to get my head around this complicated-sounding grandmother. Everything was beginning to seem so much more complicated, in fact. 'So, what do you think?' I asked. '*Do* you think she wants you to go home to her? I'm guessing she didn't tell you she was going to speak to social services?'

'No. She just said to let me know where I was staying and she'd bring Saffy over. But I didn't tell her. I knew I mustn't or,' she smiled slightly, 'you'd kick off.'

'But you told her you were in care.'

'Yes. But that was all, honest. She wanted to know where, but I never messaged back. I just got … Well, I suppose a bit edgy. It kept all coming back and I kind of wished I hadn't. I got scared.'

176

Which would perhaps explain the woman's determination to track her down via social services. Though not her motivation. That was still far from clear. 'So, do you think you want to see her? Remember, love, you don't have to.'

Elise hooked a hank of hair over her ear and lifted her chin. 'I want to see Saffy,' she said firmly. 'So yes. Yes, I think I should. But only with you there. I don't want to have to be taken off to one of those places like they took me to before.'

'You mean a contact centre? To see your gran?'

Elise shook her head. 'No, I saw Nan at home. That was when I first went to Jan's. It was Dad I had to see there because the witch wouldn't let me in the house. It was horrible. I mean, the people were nice, but it was all just so *weird*. Plus, I really want you there. Will they let her come here?'

Would they? Almost certainly. Should I offer that? I didn't know. But if I wanted to see Elise and her mother together, up close, then that was surely my best chance of doing so. 'I'm sure they will,' I told Elise. 'I'll call your social worker.'

And, hopefully, start joining a few dots.

Chapter 17

As it turned out, I didn't need to ask if Elise's mum could come to mine, as, once a date had been set for the following week, Christine Bolton asked me if I could supervise the initial contact anyway.

'Just at first,' she said. 'Obviously, they can meet at your house, maybe have a coffee or something, and then if they want to go out together, to have some time alone, then that's fine too, but have the mother bring her back to your house. Also, perhaps you and Elise could share a secret word or phrase or something, so she can let you know if she changes her mind and doesn't want to go off alone with her mum. If she does that, you can just say that you've been told that you must accompany them on the first contact.'

I had of course agreed to this, as had Elise, and now here we were, on an overcast afternoon, about an hour after school, both pacing the living room as we awaited the arrival of Mrs Blackwell. Christine had been right.

I Just Want to be Loved

Everything about the scenario felt bizarre. Elise had dashed in and got changed, doing herself up to the nines. Almost as if applying war paint – or armour? – or going out on a date. About which I didn't comment, except to say she looked nice.

But it was the mother who preoccupied my thoughts. I know as well as the next person how the law works in the UK, but I couldn't seem to shift my incredulity that I was about to play host to a woman who, if Elise *was* to be believed, was almost certainly responsible for, or at least complicit in, the kind of hidden but sadly not uncommon crimes that made most people's blood run cold. I wasn't naive either; heaven knew, I'd seen and heard some appalling stories in my time, and looked after plenty of children who were in care because they were deemed 'at risk' of sexual abuse and exploitation. But it almost beggared belief that the woman would happily breeze into my living room knowing what she'd done and, more than that, not knowing if I knew about any of it. And if so, that really was some front.

But perhaps she really was that confident that no one could touch her on any of it. I knew about the seedy world of the dark web, the anonymity, the secret networks.

Or – and I still had to at least entertain this possibility – Elise had woven the images in those photographs into yet another of her tall tales. Because if it were all true, would she really even want to face the woman? Perhaps, yes. Children are hard-wired to love their parents, after all. Even if their parents are monsters.

I had a strong memory surface, of my first foster child, Justin, who had been subjected to the very worst kind of abuse at the hands of his mother and her 'friends'. He had been so traumatised that when he was five he had burned down the family home, yet even years later, when he was with us, and right into adulthood, he'd still craved his mother's love despite what she'd put him through, and no matter how many times she rejected him.

I hadn't seen Justin in a few years now as he'd done a gardening apprenticeship and moved far away from the area. But I didn't doubt a part of him would still crave that love from the mother who'd done him such harm. But what of Elise? How did the emotional land lie there? Perhaps I'd now get an idea.

A taxi rolled up just ten minutes after the time we'd agreed, and out of the front passenger door a swathe of corn-blonde hair was the first glimpse we both had of the woman Elise hadn't seen in four years. She was tall and slender, and, from this distance, done up to the nines too, teetering on vertiginous heels as she opened the rear door of the taxi, where she bent and fiddled for some moments with a car seat.

'God!' Elise squealed just as I clocked it too. 'She's got a baby with her!' We both watched then as a little dark-haired girl, around eight, emerged via the same car door. 'OMG, and that must be Saffy,' she added. 'She's got so *tall*. She looks like me, doesn't she?'

'Why don't you go to the front door and let them in,' I suggested, reflecting on how this little half-sister hadn't even had a name before the last ten days or so. She had never been mentioned to anyone, in any context or setting – well, as far as Elise's notes went – but was a sibling she obviously had a strong bond with. Which potentially made the mess that Elise's young life already was even messier.

I lingered by the window, watching the taxi pull away and the trio come up the path. The 'baby', who seemed to be a boy, and looked around two, sat koala-style on the woman's slim hip. Her child too? I'd presumably have the answer soon enough. In the meantime I briefly took in the details. Tight black jeans, white fitted T-shirt, stiletto boots – even in summer! – and poker-straight hair, which had been dyed in the style hairdressers called ombré, as if dipped halfway into a pot of deeper colour. She was, as the saying goes, very well put together. Very expensively put together too, by the look of it. The children, in contrast, looked scruffy and unkempt. As if their outfits had been merely thrown together.

I took all this in in a matter of moments and, mindful that first impressions were only that, and not necessarily accurate, I followed Elise out into the hall to show them in.

'Mrs Blackwell,' I said, as Elise stood back and ushered them past her and through the hallway. 'Come in.'

'It's Kennedy, actually,' she said. 'I changed my name a couple of years back.' She nodded towards the little boy, presumably to convey that he was somehow relevant.

'Sorry, Mrs Kennedy,' I corrected.

'No, no, it's just Kennedy.'

Not knowing quite what to make of that (though it at least made sense of social services' inability to track down the woman), I nodded and smiled as they trooped into the living room. Elise was yet to speak, but proffered her hand to the girl, who only looked at it warily. Meanwhile, 'Kennedy' shrugged a big black suede tote bag off her free shoulder and flung it behind her to whump down onto my sofa.

Slightly stunned, I opted for my go-to opener. 'Well, it's nice to meet you,' I said. 'I'm Casey. Can I get you all a drink?'

'Oh, you superstar!' the woman said, flashing a grin at me that revealed a set of teeth that I suspected had had the same expensive treatment as the rest of her body, including, I now noticed, perhaps the boobs. 'I could actually murder a coffee, or maybe a glass of wine?' she added hopefully.

I attended to the drinks – coffee and juice, I might add – while I listened through the open doorway as mother and daughter tried to engage in awkward conversation, of the 'How are you?', 'What have you been up to?', 'Are those extensions?' variety – the latter presumably referring to Kennedy's hair. Elise was just inspecting her mother's shimmering coral talons when I re-entered the room. (How on earth did she manage childcare with nails like that?) They were sitting now in adjacent dining chairs, the toddler on Kennedy's lap, while the little girl stood close by her side, and stared silently but intently at Elise, presumably trying hard to remember her.

'So,' I said chattily, 'is this little one yours as well?'

'Yes, this is Dom,' Kennedy said, jiggling him on her knees, 'our little tyke.'

I noticed he had a worm of green snot between his nose and upper lip. He wasn't just scruffy, I realised. He was grubby. There were little half-moons of brown under his tiny fingernails and, like his sister, still in a crumpled school skirt and faded polo shirt, his mousy hair looked dull and dirty. I couldn't help but form another first impression. That the woman's extensive grooming operations clearly left no time for doing the same with her children.

'Hello, Dom,' I said, 'would you like a drink?' He nodded, but before I handed him the sippy cup of juice I'd brought in, I first went to the coffee table and grabbed the resident box of tissues. But even as I went to hand them to Kennedy, she'd already lifted up the bottom of his T-shirt, and, exposing his pale chest, wiped his nose with that instead.

'So, what do you think of your little brother?' she asked Elise brightly, while I gaped. 'He runs us ragged, doesn't he, Saff? He's quiet now, because he's in a strange place and he's not properly woke up yet, but you wait. A regular home wrecker, this one. You'll know all about that, I suppose,' she said, turning to me and grinning, slightly manically, I thought, 'being in your line of work.'

There was no side to her, but neither was there a trace of any emotion I'd normally see in a parent in this situation. Contact visits were usually strained, difficult things, with parents often strung up with guilt and anxiety or, if not, with anger and resentment (sometimes understandable and sometimes misplaced) that they no longer had agency over their own children. In Kennedy, by contrast, I saw none of that. She was as cheerful and bouncy as Elise herself had seemed that first time she arrived at our home. There was certainly no hint that she was worried about what I might know about the time Elise had spent in *her* care.

So had I been played? If so, why? It still made no sense to me. 'I do indeed,' I said, pushing a coffee across to her, and handing a beaker of juice to Saffy, who had still yet to speak, bar responding to the juice with a barely audible 'thank you'. 'Anyway, how was your journey? Have you come very far?'

'Bloody miles,' Kennedy said. 'Had to double back as it's the other way from Saffy's school. And how about you, missy?' she said, looking at Elise. 'You in school?' Elise nodded. 'Where's that, then?'

Elise glanced at me, obviously reticent about telling her mother. 'A local comp,' I said. 'And you've settled in really well there, love, haven't you?'

Another nod. She was still trying to coax her sister to come and sit by her. 'Though you're probably nearly done with school anyway now, aren't you?' said Kennedy. 'What are you now, fifteen? Sixteen?'

'*Four*teen,' Elise immediately corrected her. 'I'm not fifteen till September.' And I could so clearly see the hurt and surprise in her expression. No trace here of the girl who wanted to pass for an eighteen-year-old.

As for me, I was still trying not to spit out my coffee. Small lapses with dates happened to all of us sometimes, but to be *that* out about your own child's age? For me that spoke volumes. Why exactly *was* this woman here? I was still standing at this point, the idea being that I'd retire to a reasonable distance to give them some privacy. But noting Elise's glance in my direction I decided to initiate our 'don't let me go out with them alone' protocol, just to confirm that my instinct was correct – that despite agreeing to the meeting, and presumably being pleased to see her sister, Elise's worst fears about her mother had just been confirmed. Not that the prospect of going out looked to be on the agenda anyway. They'd come by taxi, and without a buggy, so where would they go?

I'd purposely left a plate of biscuits in the kitchen, and now I brought the code into play. 'Anyone like a biscuit?' I asked.

Elise's response was immediate. She began to stand up. 'Don't worry, Casey. I'll get them.'

I told her to stay put and I would, but that was it. My signal that Elise wanted this meeting to remain in this house and, more importantly, that she wanted me to stay right there. So, having fetched the biscuits, which Saffy declined but her brother fell upon delightedly, I pulled out another chair and sat down with them at the table.

'So,' Elise's mum said, 'it's just you doing this fostering, is it?' She was casting her gaze around the room as she spoke, her eyes moving across the rows of photos arranged on the various surfaces. 'Or do you have an other half? Children of your own?'

'Both,' I said, sad and irritated that rather than talk to her daughter she was interrogating me. 'A husband, grown-up children. Grandchildren, one son at home. Well, for now. He's moving out in a couple of weeks. Saffy?' I said, turning my attention to Elise's still mostly mute sister. 'Would you like Elise to take you to fetch some paper and felt tips? Maybe find some books for the little one too?'

Finally, the girl nodded, and allowed Elise to take her by the hand. Perhaps a few minutes alone together would bring the girl out of her shell a little. 'So, you'll miss that one,' Kennedy said, as we both watched them head off to the conservatory. The little boy was still jiggling up and down on her lap, and I realised she hadn't once seemed to sit still, her legs constantly drumming up and down beneath the table. So, *was* she nervous after all? Or was she wired? An uncomfortable thought started taking shape.

'I will indeed,' I said, pleased to hear the sound of conversation coming from the conservatory. 'It'll seem very quiet without him. But it's lovely to have Elise around.' I paused before loyally uttering what was obviously only a half-truth. 'She's always polite, and so helpful around the house too. She's really no trouble at all.'

Kennedy immediately rolled her eyes and laughed. 'Wish I could say the same! Eyes in the back of my head all the time, me, specially with this one. Anyway –' she sniffed and glanced down at the chunky gold watch on her thin wrist. 'That's life, I suppose. How long's Elise been living with you anyway? Last I heard of her she was staying with her nan. What happened there? How'd she end up in care?'

I paused for a second so I could choose my words carefully. 'Well, as far as I know, she'd been sofa surfing with various friends for a while,' I said. 'I'm not really sure about her nan as that was all before my time. She was with another foster carer before she came to me.' I stopped at that. I knew for a fact that I mustn't say any more than that and I was sure that if social services wanted Kennedy to know more, they would tell her. But despite her question she didn't really appear to be that interested – she glanced down at her watch as I was speaking, and her only response when I finished was to nod and say, 'Ah, I see,' giving me the impression that she was just making conversation.

Elise and Saffy returned from the conservatory at that point, the latter clutching one of my mindfulness colouring books and a pencil case, and Elise a couple of picture books for her brother. But even as Saffy sat back at the table and Elise held the books out to the little one, Kennedy was already pushing her chair back and thrusting the boy towards her.

'Here, can you have him, Lise? I need to spend a penny. Coffee's gone straight through me – always does, doesn't it?' she added, grinning. 'Alright to use your loo, love?'

'Yes, of course,' I said as Elise took the startled and now biscuit-chomping infant. 'Door on the left in the hall.' I noticed she scooped the bag up as she went.

Elise watched her go, her little half-brother wriggling against her, and looking over his head at me with an expression that mirrored my own. I think we were both by now struck dumb with it all.

'Here,' I said, 'let me take him. You sit down with Saffy.' Then for want of knowing quite what else to do, frankly, said, 'Little Dom and I will go and put the kettle on again.'

But the torture was to continue no longer. Having refilled the kettle, and clicked it on, I pottered in the kitchen for a bit, distracting the little one from getting fractious by helping him rearrange our fridge magnets, and having another decent go with a wet wipe on his sticky nose and mouth. Though given half a chance I would have stripped him off and bathed him in the sink. I then heard the lock on the downstairs loo go and came out to find Kennedy finally re-emerging from the toilet, wiping her nose with a bunched-up piece of loo roll.

I followed her into the living room where she now held up a bejewelled mobile phone. 'That's the taxi,' she said. 'He'll be back in five minutes.'

Elise, colouring with Saffy now, looked up at her. 'You leaving already, Mum?' she asked her, confused. 'But you've only just got here.'

'I know,' her mother said, 'but I have to get back for work. If I'd booked it for any later we'd be stuck in the rush hour, wouldn't we? And that one'll need feeding before he starts kicking off,' she added, nodding towards the infant that was still in my arms but now grizzling and reaching out towards his mother, his little fists repeatedly closing and opening.

'Can we get a Maccy's drive-thru?' the little girl asked, beginning to feed the felt pens she'd only just got out back into their case.

'Maybe,' she said. 'Anyway, nice to see you, Lise. You behave yourself, won't you?' Then, as her phone began vibrating in her hand, 'Ah, that's the cabbie. He must be outside. Come here, then, Dom-Dom.' I handed him over. 'Nice place you've got here, Lacey. Saff, you good to go?'

'Oh. Okay. I'll see you out, then,' Elise said, miserably. And as she got up from the table to follow them out into the hall, all I could think was what the hell had been going on here?

Chapter 18

As I helped Mike heave the final box into his work van, I saw that Tyler, who was busy loading Naomi's little car, had stopped and was watching me carefully.

'What's wrong?' I called, wondering if we'd been a little too robust throwing that last box in. 'That one wasn't filled with breakables, was it?'

'A bit late if it was,' Mike added, laughing.

I was taken aback then, because Tyler walked over and hugged me tightly. 'No, Mum, nothing's wrong,' he said. 'It's just I feel so lucky to have you and Dad. All this crap you have going on with Elise, and still you're helping us move to York. I hope you know how much me and Naomi both appreciate you.'

I bit my lip, hard. It wouldn't do to have a simpering breakdown just now, even though I could barely hold back the tears. I already felt as tightly coiled as a spring – I had been since I'd woken up – and I knew that this act of random tenderness could easily set me off. All I could do was try to brush it off.

'Oh behave, Ty,' I said, trying my best to laugh. 'Of course we want to help! And anyway, Dad's happy because he got to have a well-deserved Saturday off for once, so actually you're doing *us* the favour. And yes, of course I know how much it's appreciated. Now come on, if we're going to stop for brunch halfway there, we really need to get going.'

Tyler knew. He grinned and kissed my cheek. 'You're the best, Mum. We'll race you to the service station, then.'

'You bloody well won't!' I said as I watched him jump back into their car. 'Drive carefully, Naomi!'

As they drove off 'carefully' and Mike got into the driving seat of his van, I had to really give myself a good talking to, so that I didn't dissolve into an emotional wreck. 'Right, then,' I said to him, 'if we're good to go, I'll go and tell Elise we're ready.'

Though it hadn't been the original plan, Elise was coming with us to help move Tyler and Naomi to York. It had been almost a week now since that strange contact visit, and since then, apart from school, where it had been the final week of the summer term, Elise, uncharacteristically, had barely left the house. She'd been on edge the whole time, saying that she should never have agreed to see her mum, and how she especially regretted that she'd agreed to her coming to our house, because she worried that she could just show up at any time now.

And with one thing in mind, I thought. Trouble. Because it had soon become clear that my instincts about 'Kennedy' were right, which was not just a crushing blow to any lingering hopes Elise might have had about her mother's affections, but worrying evidence that she'd been motivated purely by self-interest, anxious that Elise might be intent on making trouble for *her*.

She didn't waste time making her position clear, either. The same evening of the visit, Elise had come down to me and Mike at 10 p.m., holding her phone out so we could read a short string of WhatsApp messages.

They had begun mildly enough – *I'm glad to know you've got sorted*, and, *Saffy's pleased she got to see you* – but had wasted no time in cutting to the chase; the real reason for her visit in the first place. So she could, it was so blindingly obvious to me now, better threaten her. When Elise had replied that she'd really like to keep in touch with Saffy, 'Kennedy' had come straight back with the thinly veiled threat that that would depend on her keeping her 'trap shut'. *I'm earning good money now, and I'm sorted*, she'd written, *so just a heads up – don't get any ideas about telling anyone anything. And don't think your foster carers can protect you if you do, because you know I have eyes and ears everywhere.*

Elise, sensibly, had elected not to answer that one. But even as I was reading it, another one came in. *Oh, and I forgot to mention when I came up – Uncle Max sends his love.* I handed the phone back to Elise, studying her face as I did so. '"*Uncle* Max"? Is this one of the "uncles" you told me about?' Elise nodded and snatched the phone back. 'And does he have a second name?'

Now she shook her head. 'Probably. I mean, yes, *obviously*, but even if I knew it, it wouldn't be his real one. Should I answer this? God, I can't even believe she'd *do* that.'

'No,' I said. 'Just take a screenshot of it all for me. And don't worry, love. We've got this, okay?'

But did we? I'd reported it all immediately and passed over Kennedy's phone number and the screenshot to the powers that be, but the only advice I'd been given so far was to try to keep Elise indoors and keep her off social media if I could. Yes, right! So easy to do *that*, I thought but didn't say.

In fact, as it turned out, Elise was so shaken by her mum's visit and her flurry of texts that she pretty much policed herself anyway. She said she had no intention of sending any further messages to her mum, and I believed her, my heart breaking for her as those last vestiges of hope faded away that there might have been any miraculous change in her mother, or that there was any sort of relationship between them to be reclaimed.

Since then, she'd holed up at home for the most part, brooding over the strange meeting and the emotional line she needed to draw now, but, frustratingly, even *less* inclined now than she had been to open up about her time living with her mother – not to me, and definitely not to some 'randomer', as she'd put it – convinced now that her mother would find out what she'd done and that the consequences for her little sister would be terrible.

In that respect, then, the whole 'opening up' process was beginning to look as if it had been a spectacular own goal. Because it was opening up to me about what had happened to her at her mum's that had set Elise off thinking about the little sister she'd left behind there, and which had, of course, prompted her to go searching for her mother and open up this horrible can of worms for her. And now she'd seen Saffy for herself, she was naturally even more anxious, her guilt at having left her there now acute.

But what to do? She was convinced now that she'd done the wrong thing at every turn, and that the best way to ensure nothing bad was going to happen, to either her or her sister, was to keep her head down and do as her mother said.

I'd tried logic with her – since she *was* doing that why would her mother come round and hassle her? – but now she'd opened up the hornet's nest she was beyond being rational, so all I could do was hope that the information I'd passed on would be sufficient that the woman was interviewed. At least I hoped so. Past experiences had taught me that in a situation such as this, where veiled threats or clear threats had been made towards a child, then social services had a duty of care and *must* do something. Usually, it would involve reports being made to managers, who would then decide who should go out and visit the parent and make it clear that contact like this must stop immediately. The adult involved would also be warned that a child's phone would be monitored to look out for further contact and, if deemed inappropriate, then the police would be brought in as well and any further contact would be suspended until it went to court to be officially stopped.

So that's what I hoped and expected would happen, and, in the meantime, I had decided not to push it. The real answer obviously lay in Elise agreeing to speak to CAMHS and giving them a little more to go on – something which I could only hope she'd eventually agree to – but while we waited there was little else I could do other than reassure her that she was safe, and that there was nothing her mother could do that Mike and I couldn't deal with, backed up by the authorities if necessary.

Still, she was very scared and had never seemed so much her age since she'd come to us. Given what had happened, and even though it meant Mike and my overnight stay had to be cancelled, I'd already decided we'd be taking us with her to York, but before I could even suggest it to her, she had asked me if there'd be room for her, because she was too scared to stay in the house on her own.

She jumped into the van now, in the row of seats behind us. 'You should have shouted me down earlier,' she said, as she buckled up. 'I would have helped you guys with all this.'

I Just Want to be Loved

I turned and grinned at her. 'But then who would have done your eyebrows and curled your hair?' I asked, before laughing at her hangdog expression. 'Don't stress, kiddo, I'd have called you if we'd needed a hand. We were fine.'

I really don't know what it is about travel and foster children talking more freely, but honestly it seems to happen every time. We'd been driving for about twenty minutes when Elise cleared her throat and then tapped me on the shoulder.

'They're really happy, aren't they? Ty and Naomi?' she said, sighing almost wistfully after she spoke. 'I bet you and Mike are really going to miss them. Casey, I am *so* sorry about those things I said about Tyler and his room and everything. I was just, well you know … jealous of him, I suppose, and I lashed out, and I can see now how it must have upset you.'

I turned to smile and patted her hand. 'It's okay, love,' I said. 'Forgiven and forgotten. You're right, though. I'm going to miss Tyler like mad, but at the same time I'm really happy for him so it's a bit of mixed feelings. Today is a happy day, however. I am absolutely set on it. No tears. If you see me snivelling give me a really good shake.'

'No tears?' Mike guffawed. 'Shall we take bets on that, eh, Elise?'

To which, since he was driving, he obviously couldn't have a thump, but I stored it away to administer later. Or not. Because I was determined that I wasn't going to cry. At least not where and when anyone might see me.

The next hour passed in mostly silence, Elise ear-budded up and dozing, Mike enjoying the drive and me enjoying the scenery, plus catching up on wedding ideas on the internet.

Then there was another tap on my shoulder; Elise still clearly brooding over her mother. 'What if she *does* turn up, though?' she wanted to know, apropos of nothing. 'I mean, what would you do if she came round with her heavies?'

'Heavies?' I said. 'Heavens. Is that what you're expecting?'

'Well, since she works in some nightclub, she'll know a few for sure.'

I swivelled around a little. 'Sweetie, what exactly can she do? Try not to let her get to you. It's probably all talk, and honestly, think about it – what *could* she do? It's not like she'd travel over here and drag you back off with her, is it? I think we both know that's not what this is about, love,' I added gently.

'I know that,' she said. 'But I've been thinking. She said those things to me but I think she really wants to threaten you and Mike. You know? In a roundabout way, anyway. She's probably worried that I've told you all about my past – like all the stuff that went on when I lived with her – but I haven't. Not all of it. Her threats are to warn me not to. She knows if I do, you'll report it, so she would find out, and then …'

I Just Want to be Loved

'It will all be okay, Elise,' I said. 'I promise. Just try not to think about it. I know it must be hard, but honestly, love, there's not a lot else we can do. I've told social services and they will look into it without getting you into trouble. They promised me that. They are used to things like this and they have plenty of ways and means.'

They also had a good bit to go on now. I'd spared no words in describing the state of Kennedy's children, or the way she'd been with Elise. And the way she'd been, period. I was convinced the woman must be using some kind of drugs. Probably cocaine, given her demeanour at our house, her inability to sit still or to be able to converse, or even listen, at least in a meaningful way. I was also now concerned about her statement that she was earning good money. Elise had already hinted that this was to do with something pornographic, and possibly connected to the club she also worked in, though she hadn't said how she knew this or what exactly it was. Again, I didn't push it, because I wanted her to take the lead, but whatever it was it didn't sound at all good and it seemed that mummy dearest was determined to stay in this line of work.

Like Elise, though, I took my own advice and put it out of my mind and, after brunch was called off – we decided we'd wait and have lunch in York instead – we arrived at the little apartment the kids were now renting, and my whole focus was, happily, on Ty and Naomi.

The rest of the day went really well. The little apartment that the kids were renting – the kids! I think I'll always call them that – was so much nicer than I had imagined it would be. Tiny, yes, but it had everything they needed, including built-in kitchen appliances and a microwave, a pair of no doubt trendy but definitely uncomfortable-looking sofas and a cute little pull-down dining table fixed to the kitchen wall, with a couple of stools tucked away in a corner. It was tastefully deco-rated in white and cream, and all the windows had vertical blinds. In fact, they'd need to buy nothing more than a kettle and a toaster, as the kitchen cupboards and drawers were even stocked with crockery and cutlery.

'A right bargain!' Mike declared after he'd had a thorough nosey around. 'Even the bed's got sheets and duvets! It's marvellous!'

Tyler laughed. 'You sound like a dinosaur, Dad! Almost all of the rentals round here come fully equipped – it's quite normal, you know.'

I was too busy fawning over the little blingy silver ornaments scattered on various side tables to add my thoughts on how 'dinosaur' we oldies were, but I did shake my head as Mike continued.

'You don't know you're born these days, kid,' he added. 'When me and your mum got our first place we didn't own a telly for almost a year, and all our stuff was second hand.'

'Yeah, yeah,' Tyler answered, nudging Elise so she could share the joke, 'and I bet you went out on a Friday night, paid for all your beer, got fish and chips on the way back, and still had change from a pound!'

I Just Want to be Loved

To be honest, despite Elise being so down for the last few days, she did manage to get into the spirit of the occasion and helped Naomi put all of their clothes into drawers while fighting off Tyler throwing the odd pair of socks at her. All in all, it was a really fun day and thankfully, even when the time came to leave them, I didn't feel tearful at all. Far from it, in fact. We arranged to go back up in a fortnight and treat them to the meal out we hadn't been able to have this time, and as we pulled away I was already genuinely looking forward to it – not snivelling into a tissue, as I'd expected. No doubt I'd get home, see Ty's empty bedroom and have a snivel in there instead, but that was fine. At least this hurdle – the one I'd been dreading – had been leapt.

The high spirits continued on the return journey, too, with Mike putting on one of his favourite comedy podcasts, which kept us all entertained for most of the way. It was only as we were close to home that Elise's worries surfaced again.

'Casey, one last question,' she asked me, 'then I swear I'll shut up. What if my mum demands me back? What if she says it's that section whatever, and that I have to go live with her again? Social services won't have a choice, will they? They'll have to do as she says. They'll force me to go back to her, won't they?'

I swivelled in my seat and shook my head. 'No. Not at all, love. Not at your age. They have to take on board your wishes, so even if that did happen, if you said you didn't want to, then nobody would try to force you.'

Casey Watson

'So, they can refuse, if I say so?'

'Yes, they can. Absolutely.'

That seemed to settle her slightly, but it immediately got me thinking. If Kennedy really, really pushed it, and if Elise was as afraid of her as she seemed, then actually she *could* potentially end up back with her mother, simply because she was too scared to do otherwise.

It was a scenario I'd certainly seen before. One of my best friends, Jackie, is also a foster carer and she'd been through exactly this situation with a teenage girl called Annie, who had been taken into care, aged eleven, due to neglect, and although weekly contact had been allowed and arranged, the mother never even made the first one – she just upped and left. For years, then, despite the best efforts of social services, nobody had been able to trace her.

Four years later, however, she suddenly reappeared, full of remorse and wanting only to try and patch things up with her long-lost daughter. Annie was overjoyed (children so rarely, if ever, lose that yearning or that hope), and contact was quickly re-established between them. And though the social worker and Jackie were understandably sceptical, the subsequent contact visits all went really well.

So well, in fact, that having just turned sixteen Annie announced that she was leaving care, which she had a right to do, and was going back to live with her mother. But that wasn't the end of the story. Two months after that, Jackie received a call late at night from the

Emergency Duty Team asking if they could bring Annie back to hers straight away. It transpired that poor Annie had been duped. She admitted then that she hadn't wanted to go home to her mother; she'd been manipulated by the woman using emotional blackmail, saying that if Annie didn't go and live with her she was as good as dead herself – that she was struggling with depression and had several times attempted suicide – in short, if Annie didn't come home and take care of her, it would kill her.

Such is the strength of a child's need to be loved by their parents. It wasn't long, however, before the scales fell from the girl's eyes. Her mother did need her, to help provide the means to pay for her drug habit; she would bring men home who'd pay handsomely to have sex with her daughter. So, she'd returned to Jackie, and had stayed there till she was in her early twenties, but even more scarred than she had been when she'd first come to her.

I knew Elise was vulnerable. So much more vulnerable than she herself realised. So, though I didn't exactly see her mother using those kinds of tactics, I knew just how important it was to be vigilant, and to ensure Elise felt strong enough – both in herself, and with our support – that she could stand up to her mother if it came to it.

But I also understood that primal need in a child. So, I just really hoped it wouldn't come to it.

Chapter 19

With the summer holidays now upon us, and no school routine, Elise very quickly became even more reclusive and withdrawn. And with a whole six weeks stretching ahead without any kind of structure, I could all too easily envisage her spending day after day in her room, clicking away on her phone, scrolling through social media and communicating with other people only via the internet – i.e. existing only in her virtual reality.

It was unsustainable, clearly, so, after leaving her mostly to her own devices on the Monday, on the Tuesday I tried to persuade her to come into town with me to do a bit of shopping. Clothes shopping, that is – something that would normally have teenage girls pulling on their trainers in seconds – but she wasn't interested in taking the bait.

'You go, Casey,' she said, when I went up to her room to suggest it. 'I'll stay here with the doors locked, just in case.'

'Just in case what?' I asked, obviously knowing full well what, but wanting to encourage her to vocalise her fears – to at least make inroads into having that conversation.

'Have you forgotten that Mum knows where we live?' she pointed out. 'Because I haven't. But I don't want to spoil your day,' she added. 'You go. I'll be fine. I'll just stay upstairs and keep the door locked. It's okay.'

'Elise, I'm sure she wouldn't just turn up here, not without first arranging it. And anyway, if she *did* plan on doing that, then surely you'd be better off out of the house with me anyway?'

Elise threw her arms up in the air as though I were a lost cause. 'You don't *get* it, Casey. I *know* what she's like – and she's practically said it without actually saying it. I *told* you. She *knows* people, bad people. It won't be her that comes. She's not stupid. If she thinks for one minute I might be trying to land her in it she'll send one of her cronies round to put the frighteners on instead.'

So, shopping was off. Though technically she was old enough to be left at home, there was no way I'd do that – not when she was feeling so vulnerable and scared.

But what was to be done? I'd passed on everything I knew, plus had outlined my own concerns, but there was little anyone could do to provide Elise with reassurance and, whatever Christine and I thought about what Kennedy might get up to, we weren't living in the sort of science-fiction movie where people could be arrested on the basis that they *might* commit a crime. I was sure social services would be looking into it, particularly in relation to the safety of her other children, but where Elise herself was concerned all I could practically do was keep reassuring her that Mike and I would protect her.

I was relieved, then, to hear from Holly Davies that lunchtime.

'I know it's not Friday,' she said, after I caught her up on the current situation, 'and I know it doesn't exactly fit in with my usual nine-to-five visits, but how about I take Elise out tonight for that curry I promised her? I could collect her around six, if that's okay? And, of course, you can come too, if you like.'

'I like,' I said. 'Will be good to get her out of the house. If she'll agree to it, that is. It's all well and good us all telling her not to be afraid, and to carry on regardless, but if she's that fearful of her mother then of course it's going to fall on deaf ears.'

'If it's any consolation, we are doing our best behind the scenes, Casey. Though to be honest, I'm not sure there's much more to say right now. Someone did speak to Elise's mother after the visit, but it seemed pretty clear that she had no interest in seeing Elise again. So, I suspect you might be right in thinking she was essentially just checking up on her, which fits with the idea that she's worried about the possibility that Elise might disclose things she doesn't want disclosing. So that might well be it – a bit of hot air to make the girl think twice about doing so. But, like you say, even if we assume her threats have no real substance, poor Elise can't be sure, can she? And we both know what she needs to do if we're to have any teeth with this – be prepared to speak out about what she knows. Anyway, let me think some more and I'll try to have a plan for when we meet later. That okay?'

It was more than okay by me, and, to my delight, Elise too. Especially when I told her I'd be coming along too.

'I don't have eyes in the back of my head, Casey,' she explained, 'and you've met my mum, so you'd recognise her if she walked in and I had my back to her or something.'

Which was patently not going to happen. Did she assume Kennedy's henchmen would have us followed to the restaurant? But when I put that to her, her response was unequivocal. That she might well do exactly that. 'She knows some very bad people,' she said. 'You don't realise.' Which made me wonder just how much we still didn't know about Kennedy, and whether her threats had been more substantive than Elise had let on. So I could only hope Holly would have better luck than I did in persuading her that the best way forward was for her to share everything she knew.

By 5.45 p.m. Elise finally descended from her bedroom, dressed up to the nines, and with a full hair and face makeover. Normally I would have suggested that going to the local curry shop called for a more dress-down dress code, but I was so relieved to see she'd made an effort for the first time in days that I went a bit overboard in gushing about how beautiful she looked. Which seemed to please her.

'Thanks, Casey,' she said, walking across the room to check the window. 'I didn't want to show you up so I did my best. Are we going in your car or Holly's?'

'I didn't think to ask,' I said, 'but I'm fine either way. Probably mine, though, as I know where we're going. Holly probably doesn't know the area that well yet.'

I was wrong, though. Holly had obviously done her research. 'Hop in,' she said, leaning over to open the passenger door. 'I've Googled it. Spice Garden is already in my sat nav and my belly is rumbling at the thought of that delicious menu, so let's go, girls.'

It was quite a change for me, going out to eat during the week, and though I'm a wimp when it comes to curry – butter chicken is about the spiciest I can manage – it was good to see both the girls tucking in with gusto, and to observe how easily the conversation flowed. The topics were wide-ranging – from the merits of this or that make-up brand, to fast fashion, to the subjects Elise most enjoyed in school. It was only when the food was gone and the waiter had brought us coffees that Holly steered the conversation round to Elise's mother.

'I've been thinking, Elise,' she said, after taking a sip from her coffee. 'Casey was saying that you genuinely believe that your mum might do something bad, like have you followed, or send someone to the house to threaten you or something. Is that correct?'

Elise's chin jutted. 'She might. And I'm not lying, honestly. My mum's dangerous, she really is, and I'm really scared for Saffy. She's my sister, and even if she doesn't remember me, I need to protect her. I was about her age when I went back there and all the shit started happening. But I don't know what to do about it. What *can* I do?'

Holly nodded. 'I hear you. You must feel damned if you do and damned if you don't, right?' Elise nodded. 'And I'm also beginning to understand just how afraid you are for your little sister. But you know what? The very *best* thing you could do to protect her is to speak out. To tell people very truthfully about what happened to you as a child and how you're afraid that history will repeat itself. Do you get that?'

Elise's eyes filled with tears now. 'I'm too scared to,' she said. 'And who would I tell anyway? And no one will believe me even if I *do* tell. They never did before. And Mum will find out, and then –'

'You've spoken about what happened at your mum's before, Elise?'

She nodded. 'To a teacher.'

'When was this, love?' I asked her. Elise's file was full of instances where she'd 'told', about one thing or another, but in every case it had ended with no further action – usually because it turned out to be unsubstantiated. There was nothing on her file about her time at her mum's, I was sure.

'When I was living there. I told my teacher at the primary school I was going to.'

'And nothing happened?' Holly asked.

Elise shook her head. 'Least, I don't know. We moved then. To a new flat, somewhere else. I never went back there. I stopped going to school then.'

I had three school uniforms and no bloody school. I caught Holly's eye as I took Elise's hand. 'Oh, sweetheart,' I said. 'You must have felt so abandoned.'

I had a thought then. Those horrible photographs. 'Sweetheart,' I added. 'Those photos I saw. Did you show them to anyone back then?'

She shook her head. 'No. And that's *exactly* why I took them.'

'Took them?' Holly asked.

'When I ran away from Mum's. I got them out of the stash for posting out to people. Customers. I wanted *proof.*'

But she had never used them, sadly. How different things might have been if only she'd showed them to her nan. But there was nothing to be done now, so all I could do was squeeze her hand.

Holly leaned forward. 'Elise, I absolutely *promise* you that if you speak with CAMHS and tell them everything, they *have* to act, it's their job. I don't know how what happened happened – I imagine your mum must have moved away and taken you out of school precisely

I Just Want to be Loved

because you spoke out – but CAMHS absolutely cannot sit back and do nothing if they suspect your siblings are in danger. But they cannot help unless they have your testimony. I know you're frightened, but telling the truth about what happened to you is the one way you *can* help protect your sister. You didn't have a big sister to look out for you when you were Saffy's age, but you can be there for her now. You *can* do that thing for her.'

'But what if they don't believe me? And what if they tell Mum I told? What's to stop her disappearing again, with Saffy?'

What indeed? I thought. If you were savvy, and this Kennedy clearly was, it would be all too easy for her to slip through the net again. Without tangible evidence, and given Elise's history of crying wolf, it would be all too easy to present herself, and her children, in such a way that suspicions would only ever be that – suspicions.

'I hear you,' Holly said again. 'But will you at least think about it?'

To which Elise responded with a promise that she would. Which, for now at least, was the best we could hope for. We both knew it might take days for Elise to overcome her many reservations, and when Holly dropped us off we exchanged a few words to that effect. She'd visit again, she said, on Friday, and see if she could make any further progress, and till then all I could do was keep doing what I was doing and not pressure her too much. When it came, if it came, it would have to be from her.

I was shocked, then, when she appeared in the kitchen, close to eleven that evening, her face pale but her expression firmly set.

'I've decided. I need to tell someone. *Now*,' she said.

Say what you like about staffing cuts and budget cuts and the enormous backlog of cases, but sometimes the state does come good. Galvanised by the look of firm resolve on Elise's face that night, first thing the following morning I called Holly, who called CAMHS, and then gave me another number – a hotline, if you like – which I called and who offered us an emergency appointment, not even twenty-four hours later.

I was now sitting on an uncomfortable square-shaped red chair in the CAMHS offices, waiting to be called in. I had never been here before. The last time I'd taken a child to a CAMHS appointment it had been in a dilapidated old building, not very far from home, which consisted of three consulting rooms and a tatty reception. I think the building, given the décor, had previously been a guest house, and not a particularly high-end one, either.

I hadn't taken many children there – most appointments tended to be conducted at my home – so hadn't even realised the old place had disappeared now, much less that they'd built (or were renting) this swanky new place, out of town. Which, looking around me, I wasn't sure I much liked. The primary colours were garish, the lights way too bright and, worst of all, all the walls had been adorned with bits of modern art, mostly in the shape of rather wishy-washy abstract prints on top of which sat inspirational quotes. I got what they were thinking, but for me it just jarred. No child or teenager in the midst of profound emotional trauma was likely to get one iota of solace or comfort from being told to 'seize the day' or to 'look through the rain to see the rainbow'.

Elise was currently in with the counsellor. She'd said nothing more to me about the reason for her sudden decision, only that she was determined to protect her sister, and I gave a silent prayer of thanks that Holly had been so upfront with her in pointing out that she could be the person for Saffy that she herself had never had, which would have definitely given her food for thought. I also felt really relieved that they'd booked her in so quickly. Experience had taught me that, despite good intentions, if a teenager was left for a long period of time after a disclosure, they became less inclined to speak about it again. I had desperately hoped that Elise would agree and not cancel yet another session, but thankfully she had agreed to it. If anything, she was even more determined than when she had instigated it. She had just made me promise not to go anywhere.

And that was what I'd done. The only fly in the oint-ment had been that I had been told very firmly that I couldn't accompany Elise into the consultation room itself – not at first, anyway. The appointment was booked for an hour and I was told that after around forty-five minutes someone would come out for me and I could join them then.

I was reading one of the posters on the reception wall for the umpteenth time – a mind map of mental health issues – when a young woman stood up from behind a glass panel at the reception desk and waved across to get my attention.

'Mrs Watson?' she asked. 'They're ready for you now. I'll press the buzzer to allow you through. Straight down the corridor, third door on the left.'

Gathering up my jacket and bag, I headed towards the corridor I'd watched Elise go down earlier, with the counsellor, and, when the buzzer sounded, walked through the security gate. (These seemed mandatory now, probably a sign of the times, though it was also possibly because a lot of the young people who were seen here were psychologically troubled enough to have been sectioned.)

The counsellor smiled up at me now. Her name was Ellie, and she had a distinct air of calm and sagacity about her. I put her somewhere in her thirties, and I wondered what had brought her to this line of work. I knew lots of CAMHS counsellors had a lifelong passion for what they did, often coming here via work in prisons, specialist hospitals and children's homes.

'Casey,' she said, 'lovely to meet you at last. Please take a seat.' She indicated the vacant armchair next to Elise.

I Just Want to be Loved

I sat down, took the hand Elise held out to me, and squeezed it, touched at her instinctive need to reach out to me for physical comfort. 'You okay, sweetie?'

She nodded but her eyes were red-raw from crying. She looked shattered, in fact, almost as if she'd been in a physical fight. 'I will be,' she said. I felt the pressure of her own hand in mine now. 'And I want you to know everything.' She glanced over at the counsellor. 'Ellie said it's my choice, and I want you to know.'

'You can share as little or as much as you like, love,' I told her. 'I'm just happy that you're here and can start to get some help.'

'And that's what she will get,' Ellie said firmly. 'And perhaps I can get you up to speed a bit first, Casey. Elise tells me she's told you a lot about her childhood, but not all. Today she has disclosed that she was sexually assaulted many times when she lived with her mother, almost all of the perpetrators being male friends of hers. Elise tells me that she is sure her mother knew about almost all of them and would tell her to keep her mouth shut if she tried to complain about it. There are many bad memories,' she glanced over at Elise, 'and Elise is allowing me to write them up and share them all with you, which I will do by the end of today. Far more pressing, however, are the worries she currently has about her little sister Saffy, and quite possibly the baby too.'

I nodded. 'I appreciate that,' I told her. 'And, yes, I'm aware that Elise is worried about Saffy and what might be happening to her too.'

Elise gripped my hand again. 'I'm so sorry I didn't tell you before,' she said. 'Just saying it out loud was too scary. It would make it real and I didn't want it to be. But now I know it is.' She lifted her phone from where it had been sitting in her lap. 'I have evidence. Look.'

Letting my hand go, she pressed the screen a couple of times and pulled up a photograph. She then handed me the phone so I could see better. I recognised Saffy immediately, in a picture that had been taken in a restaurant. She was sitting at a table, a meal having obviously just been eaten – there were empty plates, glasses, half a pizza and a cutting wheel left on a wooden board – and beside her, his arm loosely around her shoulder, was a man.

He looked around forty. He was dressed in a grey suit and white shirt, and his hair, which was dark brown, was shiny and styled. A short goatee beard covered his chin. He looked carefree and happy and perfectly decent. That was until you looked a little closer. At the child beside him, whose smile was immediately arresting, by virtue of the fact that it didn't reach her eyes. By the fact that it looked pasted on. She was smiling for the camera, but her expression was haunted. It's a word I use a lot in relation to children – at least *some* children, the kind I see more than my share of – and I know it when I see it. I was seeing it now.

'That's "Uncle" Max,' Elise said, her lip curling as she put the 'Uncle' bit in finger quote marks. 'I found this on Facebook. As soon as Mum mentioned him I felt sick to my stomach, just knowing that he was still around. It took me ages to find this but as soon as I saw it I knew … That's when I knew I had to tell someone.'

I passed the phone back. I felt sick to my stomach as well now. The child was eight, the age Elise had been when she'd been taken to her mother's. How much had she already endured at the hands of this man? How much, for that matter, had Elise?

'Elise has done well,' Ellie said now. 'To amass so much information.' She went on to explain that, using her instincts and social media experience, Elise had managed to put together quite a case. Knowing her mother had changed her name, she instinctively knew that the woman would almost certainly have created other Facebook, Instagram and possibly Twitter accounts, too, and she set about systematically tracking them down. Her hard work paid off. Within an hour she had found three of them, all with different avatars, and it was on one of these accounts that the photo had turned up. If nothing else, I marvelled at the sheer arrogance of the woman in putting photos on social media for all to see. Or perhaps she was just very naive.

'Mum is still a prostitute,' Elise said. 'Just the way she's dressed on her photos, and the stuff she says on there. Also, it's all men. No women or girls at all as friends. On Insta, she has literally *thousands* of followers. I didn't go through all of them, but, again, they're all men.'

'And this Max,' I said, glancing at Ellie. 'He's identifiable?'

Ellie shook her head. 'Not yet. He isn't tagged in the photograph. But it's him,' she glanced at Elise again, 'who Elise has disclosed was the man who had regularly abused *her*.'

'He is a monster!' Elise said, her voice high and urgent. 'You have to find him before he does the same to Saffy as he did to me!' She sobbed then. 'God, why didn't I do something *sooner*?!'

'Sweetheart,' I soothed, pulling her towards me and putting my arms around her. 'You didn't *know*. How could you? And you're here now. That's what matters.' I leaned back so I could meet her eyes. 'That you're helping Saffy *now*.'

Chapter 20

Often, at training days, or our occasional informal meet-ups, we foster carers can be found grumbling at one another about how we put forward information to our managers and then are left twiddling our thumbs while we wait to see results – often for what feels like forever. It's only natural, I suppose, to expect things to happen quickly, especially if we've forwarded particularly worrying disclosures. And if this has happened following a period of heightened emotion and trauma, then being left hanging, usually in the dark about what, if anything, is happening, can feel like an anti-climax, and very frustrating. I often compare the feeling to that which a paramedic must feel after attending a road traffic accident and administering life-saving care. The adrenaline and tension at the time must be huge for them, but then they have to leave their patient at Accident and Emergency and drive away, often never finding out the end result.

It's not quite that bad for us, of course, because in the end we usually do get to see the results; that is, for the child in our care, at least, and what it means for them. But we're not always told about what happens to any family members or other adults involved. A good line manager, at such times, is a blessing, because they will phone up at a later date and quietly tell us just enough so we know that justice has been served, even though they're really not obliged to.

Thankfully, my supervising social worker, Christine Bolton, is one of those 'good' line managers, and I was updated about the disclosures Elise had made to CAMHS within twenty-four hours. Which was, frankly, a great relief because I was already feeling sick with anticipation and could only imagine how distressing it must have been for her. I'd also elected not to read Ellie's report. At least, not yet. I already knew the substance of what would be in it, and I knew I couldn't stomach the detail.

'Oh, thank goodness, Christine,' I said as soon as I answered my mobile phone the following morning, having passed everything on to her the night before. 'It's so good to hear from you. Did you get my notes? Have you heard anything?'

I was in the kitchen with Elise, whose ears had obviously pricked up now. 'What's happened?' she asked me. 'Have they found him yet?'

'Is that Elise?' Christine asked. 'If it's just you and her, Casey, can you put me on speaker for a few minutes, so I can fill you both in? Then we'll have a chat between ourselves afterwards, if that's okay?'

'Okay,' I said, clicking on the phone icon. 'Elise, it's Christine. She's going to tell us what's been happening.'

'Hi, guys,' Christine said. 'Elise, I know you must be going out of your mind with worry, so I thought I'd call to let you know what's happened since your appointment yesterday. I hope you don't mind that what you said had to be shared with other professionals.'

'No, that's fine,' she said. 'The lady already told me that would happen. Where's my sister now? Are she and Dom okay?'

'They are indeed,' Christine said. 'Their local social services and the police went to see your mum yesterday afternoon, and besides the information that came from you, conditions were bad enough at the house that they felt justified in removing the children. They are now in a foster placement together.'

I watched Elise's eyes fill with tears. 'But are they okay, though? Oh God, what have I done? They must be so scared.'

I propped my phone up against the fruit bowl on the table and pulled my chair next to Elise so I could comfort her. So many conflicting emotions, I knew, would be churning around inside her, just as they had been all the previous evening, as the enormity of what she'd done, and set in motion, had begun to sink in. I think a part of her, even if a tiny part, wanted for this not to happen. It was the final piece in a particularly grim jigsaw, after all. 'You did the right thing, sweetie,' I reassured her. 'And see? You *were* right. Christine has just said that they needed to remove the children anyway – not just because of the things you spoke about yesterday, but because she wasn't taking proper care of them. You did the *right thing*,' I said again. 'And though, yes, I'm sure they *will* be scared, they are in a safer place, a better place, and they *will* settle, I promise you.'

'Casey's right,' Christine added. 'And they are with *such* a lovely couple. Their own children are grown up now, and they are very experienced carers. And so loving. They will take *very* good care of them.'

I passed Elise a tissue and she blew her nose and wiped her eyes. 'And Uncle Max? Have they got him?'

Christine paused before answering. 'Not yet. The priority was obviously first to get the children to safety, and the man you identified wasn't at your mum's house. But his name is in the system –'

'What does that mean?'

'That the police are involved now, and as far as I know he is part of their enquiries, as someone they are very keen to interview. I know that's not what you wanted to hear, but I'm afraid these things can take a little more time. I promise you, though, if I hear anything at all, I will make sure you know about it. Now, is there anything you wanted to ask, Elise, before I have a quick word with Casey? We've got some boring admin to do.'

'Does my mum know? You know, that I spoke to that lady?'

'No. As of this moment your mum doesn't know you've told us anything. Though she might suspect something, obviously, given how recently she saw you. So, it's really important, and I can't emphasise this enough, that you block her today from all your social media accounts. You mustn't communicate with her at *all*. Can I trust you to do that?'

Elise nodded at me. 'Yes. I'll do that. I don't want to have anything more to do with her, *ever*. But what about Saffy? Can I see her? And Dom?'

'Of course you can, sweetheart. And as soon as we can arrange it. We'll let them get settled in, then we'll arrange for you to go there and visit them. And regularly, from then on, if that's what you'd like.'

'I would *so* like. Thank you so much.'

'Thank *you*, Elise. For what you did. It was incredibly brave of you. And if you have any more questions, just ask Casey, okay? She can always check with me if she needs anything clarified. In the meantime, I need to run through some stuff with her. Is that okay? And remember to block your mum, yes? Oh, and anyone else you think might be in touch with her.'

'I will,' Elise promised her. 'I'll go and do that now, then.'

I nodded. 'And I'll be done soon,' I told her. 'I'll come up and fetch you.' I gave her a quick hug before she left.

Once she'd gone, Christine explained that before anything could be done about this Max fellow, the police were going to need to interview both Saffy and Elise. She told me to expect a call from them to arrange this for Elise, and to prepare her to have to undergo yet another emotional interview that would almost certainly involve her talking about the same very uncomfortable memories.

'What happens to that man will definitely depend on both Elise being very clear about what he actually did to her,' Christine said, 'and her sister too, of course – though fingers crossed, obviously, there will be little to tell there – because without that, they'll have nothing to go on, especially if their mother is covering up for him.'

'Don't worry,' I told her, 'I'll make sure Elise knows how important this part is. Are the kids somewhere nice? I bet they're terrified.'

'Well, obviously I won't have much to do with them as they've been placed in another local authority, but I've spoken to their social worker and apparently they are doing fine. Early days, of course, and I'm sure the little one particularly is completely disorientated, but they're still young enough to be able to get over all of this. I feel so bad for them, though – you know, neither has a father's name recorded on their birth certificates, and apparently no other family whatsoever.'

'Just awful,' I agreed. 'But at least they have Elise now.' And her them, I thought. Potentially, at least, it would be such a precious family bond. I could only hope and pray that the contact could be maintained. 'On which note, I'll get off, then, and start preparing Elise. I'll call you if she's thought of any other questions.'

Christine assured me that she'd keep her phone close to hand, just in case, and when I hung up I made myself a coffee before going upstairs to knock at Elise's bedroom door. When I went in she was sitting cross-legged on her bed with her biscuit tin on her lap, and in her hand was one of her childhood photos; one of the normal ones, that is.

'I just realised,' she said, sniffing as she handed it to me, 'apart from the dark hair, Saffy looks so like I did at her age, doesn't she? I just hope to God she hasn't had the same experiences I did.'

I sat down beside her and squeezed her arm. 'Whatever happened, and let's hope nothing has yet, you have saved her now. Just remember that, okay?'

'I'm glad they're in care now,' she said. 'I know that's a stupid thing to say about your sister and brother, but I really am. I wonder what the bad living conditions actually were at Mum's. Did Christine tell you?'

I thought back to some of the homes I had seen over the years. Filthy, dirty houses, rooms covered in animal and human excrement. Alcohol, overflowing ashtrays, no food in the cupboards. I shuddered to think about what the police might have found. But I didn't actually know.

'Christine didn't say,' I told Elise. 'But they probably didn't tell her everything. It's a different local authority, so Christine won't be working that closely with them.'

'I wish *I'd* been taken into care when I was Saffy's age,' Elise mused. 'But I loved my dad. Life was okay. We were okay. *I* was okay. It was fine till the witch stepmother showed up and ruined everything.'

I privately doubted that – it didn't fit with Elise's case notes by a long chalk. But I understood. She had rewritten history to make it less hard to revisit. To make it that bit easier to forgive her dad for letting her go. She had a point, too. Had he not been able to track down her mother, perhaps she would have ended up in the care system then, and been spared two years of hideous abuse. But what was done was done. 'Does she have a name, this witch stepmother?' I asked.

'April. I mean, *really*? What kind of a name is that? I mean, it makes her sound nice, and she is *so* the complete opposite.' She took the picture back from me and placed it in the tin, then picked up the lid, and closed it carefully. It was such a tender gesture, and I understood how much emotion lay behind it. 'I wish I hadn't been so awful to my nan. And I was,' she said. 'I was awful. I mean really, *really* awful. I was toxic. And I don't even know why. I mean, she couldn't have done more for me. And I played her up something shocking. I was foul to her. It's no wonder she couldn't cope with me.'

I reached out and took her hand. 'Don't be too hard on yourself, love,' I said. 'You had been through so much by the time you found your way there. And look at you now. You've grown up so much in the last few months.' I turned to face her. 'You know, if you wanted to start seeing your nan again, I'm sure Christine could help us facilitate that, or Holly perhaps. Is that something you would want to happen now?'

Her eyes widened. '*God*, yes. But I just can't see it happening. I mean, the last thing I said to my nan was that she should go and F-U-C-K herself. I mean, as in I really yelled it at her. And all because she wouldn't give me a tenner to go buy a McDonald's. If I was Nan I'm not sure I would want to see me again. I was *so* bad. What if she isn't ready to give me a second chance? My dad too, you know. I mean I don't know if it's all this that's made me think about everything – Saffy and Dom being put into care and stuff – but it's really got me thinking. D'you think she might forgive me?'

'Well, there's only one way to find out, isn't there? I can't speak for your nan, of course, but if it was me … then I'd *definitely* want to see you. And I'd definitely forgive you. You know, you're obviously thinking back to all the things you did, but your nan probably looks back at some of ways she reacted and, pound to a penny, I'll bet she has her regrets too. It goes with the territory – as the adult, I'm sure there would be a part of her that thinks she's failed you. As I'm sure does your dad …'

'You think my *dad* might want to see me?'

I could have bitten my tongue. I was getting into difficult territory. I had no idea if Elise's dad even gave her a second thought. And I really didn't want to get her hopes up if there were none.

'I don't know,' I said honestly. 'But let's start with your nan, yes?'

'And if she'll see me, I could at least tell her I'm sorry. And she might know whether Dad might be interested in seeing me …' She chewed her lip. 'Or not. But at least then I'd *know* …'

Such a lot of emotions for Elise to be dealing with, and I absolutely understood why she was suddenly being flooded with them, so I was thrilled when I phoned Christine back an hour later and she thought it was a great idea to try to get Elise reconciled with her grandmother.

'And we could work with Dad too,' Christine said, 'see if he's ready to try again – you never know, do you? God, Casey, wouldn't it just be wonderful if we can get them back together?' She let out a short laugh. 'Listen to me! Get thee back to the real world, Mrs Bolton! Anyway, it will be Holly that sorts all of this out,' she added. 'Give me a couple of days to get the ball rolling and I'm sure she'll ring you once she's spoken with Mrs Blackwell. In the meantime, good luck with the police when they come and let me know how Elise gets along.'

I hadn't even spoken to the poor girl about the police interview yet. And wouldn't just yet. The way I figured, one piece of shocking news in a day was about all she could deal with. That was a hurdle I'd have to cross tomorrow.

Chapter 21

Things started to happen very quickly then, and in all areas of Elise's life. First was a phone call from Holly, to let us know that Elise and her paternal grandmother were to have a contact visit. No promises, no plans and no getting up of hopes yet, but at least the woman wanted her granddaughter back in her life, which was welcome new indeed.

'Mrs Blackwell wants it to be at her house,' Holly explained, 'as she's recently been discharged from hospital after her knee op, so she can't easily get to the contact centre, but she does want me to be there to supervise the first visit.'

I was surprised at that, because in my experience, parents and grandparents usually hated the idea of a fully supervised contact in this kind of situation, saying it felt unnatural and contrived and that they didn't feel able to be themselves. I said as much to Holly now.

'I know,' she said, 'but Elise, by the sounds of it, really did give her poor nan an absolute hell of a time when she was living there.'

'I know,' I said. 'She told me. And she's keen to put that right.'

'That's good to hear,' Holly said, 'but I think she's right to have me there. Given the background, and don't forget the Elise she remembers was a very different animal to the one we're seeing now, Mrs Blackwell feels that rather than risk any allegations or confrontations, she'd feel a lot more at ease if someone is there to witness the meeting. Though she did at least say that if all goes well – and she says she's sure she'll know – that future visits could be just the two of them.'

'I'm sure Elise will understand,' I said. 'I'll just be honest with her. She's old enough to take that. And she actively wants to say sorry to her nan. And what about Dad? Any joy there yet?'

'Nope,' Holly said, sighing. 'I've left him loads of text messages, and even dropped a letter round to his house in case I'd got the wrong number, but he still hasn't been back in touch. I think that one's a bit more complicated, given everything that's happened. Still, never give up hope, eh? There's time, I suppose.'

It was disappointing about Dad, but not unexpected, and, in any case, even before the visit with Elise's grandmother would take place, there was first the gruelling business of Elise having to revisit much of what she'd told the CAMHS psychologist, only this time in front

of two police officers, because without an official statement, made *to* the police, the Uncle Max character, who
was invading my dreams now, couldn't be arrested or
charged.

Needless to say, on the day of the police visit, which
took place the following week, Elise was in a state of
high anxiety and agitation – as if it was her, and not that
monster, who was in the dock. This was such a familiar
state of affairs when it came to abused children, and
about which I would never stop feeling furious, having
sat with too many kids now, faced with reliving their
worst nightmares, and the feelings of guilt and shame
which, though groundless – they were the *victims* –
almost always threatened to overwhelm them.

But at least I was able to be present. And happily –
though I knew it shouldn't really make a difference – both
the officers who I showed into our living room were
female and I could see, just on those very unreliable first
impressions, were experienced in this uniquely sensitive
and difficult line of work. At their suggestion, they took
up positions next to one another on the sofa, while Elise
sat curled up in Mike's oversized armchair, and I
stationed myself at the dining table, where I was slightly
apart but Elise could clearly see me.

'I'm Sally, and this is Eva,' the older of the two intro-
duced herself. 'And I gather you know why we're here?'
Elise nodded, and the officer went on. 'Well, once we're
all ready, it will be me doing all the talking.' She smiled
then and added, 'Simply because I like to talk – as Eva

will attest to – but that's how it will work; it'll be me asking all the questions and Eva will be writing everything down on her iPad.'

'iPad?' Elise asked, clearly impressed. 'Is that what you use now?'

'Certainly is,' Sally answered, grinning as she looked in my direction. 'Gone are the days when we'd scribble everything down in huge notebooks and write it up in our best handwriting later. We're all very tech savvy these days – even in the police. You can even squiggle your signature on the bottom with your finger after you've read it through.'

'Well, at least *I'm* tech savvy,' Eva quipped. 'Sally has no idea how to even turn the thing on, and don't even get me started on her attempts at TikTok!'

I realised that all of this was an attempt to try and set Elise at ease, and from what I could see it was definitely working. So, I sat back a little, feeling at least reasonably confident that she was in a good enough place to go through it all again. Well, at least as good as it ever could be.

Not that it made for comfortable listening. I was mainly there to support Elise and in a listening capacity, but it was just heartbreaking to hear as she relayed her past life to the officers, stopping only to compose herself from time to time, as the full force of the memories threatened to overwhelm her for a second time. And no wonder, because her testimony made for grim listening – so much so that I wished I'd had the stomach to read the CAMHS write-up before this, so I'd at least have been partly prepared.

The man known as 'Uncle Max' – one of several men who were regularly round at the house, making indecent images and video clips for sale and pay-per-view online – had systematically groomed and abused Elise for months during her time living with her mother. He'd started predictably, by buying her sweets and toys, and then encouraging her to sit on his lap as she played. He knew her mother was a prostitute and had to go out at nights to earn her money for drink and drugs, and he made sure he was regularly on hand to babysit. At first Elise had loved the attention and the fun times she had with him, but pretty soon this had turned to horror as he began to carry her upstairs some nights, to bath her and put her to bed. This was when the touching had started and, without knowing how, she had just known it was wrong.

'I could deal with doing the pictures,' she told the police officers, 'because it was, like, just dressing up and posing the way they told you, but I always knew what was going to happen when we were left on our own because of the way he'd wink at me, if Mum was off putting Saffy to bed or something, and saying how he'd have a "special treat" for me later on.'

Uncle Max wasn't stupid, though. He took care to combine his 'special treats' with threats, making it clear to Elise that if she told anyone about it, it would be the worst thing she could do, as she would be taken away to a children's home and never see her mother or sister again. But he needn't have worried; the one time she did speak to her mother, after he'd hurt her quite badly, she was told in no uncertain terms to stop making things up, and that she should consider herself lucky to have such a generous man in her life to buy her nice things. And perhaps Mum, being a sex worker, genuinely believed that the trade-off was one worth accepting.

If that made me feel sickened, so did what came next – Elise plucking up the courage to tell a teacher what was happening, though, couched as it was, in a ten-year-old's language, I suspect it might not have been red-flagged sufficiently. Had it been picked up, how very different things could have been. As it was, she had clearly fallen through the cracks. It was possible her mother had had a visit, and perhaps we'd find that out in time, but whatever happened, all Elise knew was that they moved home soon after, and that she didn't go to school again (any school, that is – she just dressed up in school uniforms) till she finally ran away, and once she'd turned eleven, her nan enrolled her in the local high school.

But the damage to Elise's sense of trust was profound and life-changing. Twice she'd spoken out and twice no one had listened. And, worse than that, she'd been so traumatised that she'd essentially become numb, and soon made the connection between using your assets – i.e. your body – and getting things you wanted and people to bend to your will. And in her case, I suspected, as I watched her relive all those horrors, what she wanted, *all* she wanted, was to be seen and acknowledged, to get attention, for someone to love her.

'What about Saffy?' Elise asked, once she'd finished recounting her story.

The officer called Eva reassured her. 'We've already had a conversation with Saffy,' she told her, 'and with what you've told us today we are confident that we are going to be able to find him and make him pay for his abuse.'

'Did she say anything?' Elise wanted to know. 'Did he do things to her too?'

Eva looked uncomfortable and glanced at me before answering. 'I'm so sorry, Elise. I know it must be worrying for you, but I'm not allowed to say anything about your sister's statement. I'm sure, in time, the two of you will speak about it together. All I can say for the moment is that Saffy is fine now, she really is.'

I knew by the officer's face that the answer was actually yes. The man obviously *had* done things to poor Saffy, but I also knew she was right – she wasn't at liberty to discuss the ins and outs of it with Elise. All I'd be able to do was to try and reassure her that Saffy would be okay.

'And are *you* okay, love?' I asked her, once I'd shown the officers out and tried to do exactly that. 'That must have been pretty gruelling to go through again.'

'I'm okay, actually,' she said, surprising me. 'Now it's done. Now it's over. I feel … I don't know. Like I'm floating, you know?'

I nodded. 'Like a weight has been lifted from you, I'm sure.'

She shook her head, though. 'Not exactly that. I mean, yes, maybe, kind of. But more I'm floating *above* it. Like I've left it. Left *her*. Like I don't have to think about it anymore, ever. Like I can let her go now.'

Though I understood where Elise was coming from – put the past in a mental box, with a very strong padlock – I had my doubts that it would all be as easy as she'd suggested – my hunch was that the reverse would be true. There would probably be all sorts of horrors still to unpick as she navigated her way through the next part of her life and the ghosts from the past continued to haunt her. But I was glad she felt lighter of heart now she'd done it, and could only hope that she'd get the support she would need to continue to come to terms with what had happened to her.

For now, though, I was glad that in telling her story she might have saved her sister (and perhaps her brother, too) from enduring a similar fate. It could not be underestimated what a positive effect that would have on her, both in knowing she'd taken action to protect her half-siblings and, hopefully, once they understood why they'd had to leave their mother, in creating an enduring bond between them all. But there was another bond I was even more anxious about

re-cementing, and that was the one with her grandmother.

'I'm so *nervous*,' Elise said as she stared out of the
living-room window two days later, waiting for Holly to
arrive to pick her up. 'I was such a horrible little cow to
Nan. I'm still amazed she wants anything to do with
me, to be honest.' She turned to look at me. 'Do you
really think she'll have forgiven me?'

'Of course she will have,' I reassured her. 'She's your
nan, darling, and she loves you unconditionally.' I could
only trust my instinct that that was true. 'Yes, she'll have
been angry and hurt at the time because she only wanted
what was best for you, but *of course* you're forgiven. She
wants to see you, doesn't she? And to spend time with
you, too. So stop fretting. And just be yourself. Try not
to think about what's happened before.'

Elise shook her head and said, wisely, I thought, 'I
can't do that. I can't act like none of it ever happened.
I'm going to let her know how sorry I am about all the
things I did back then, and tell her how much I love and
miss her.'

'That's a lovely attitude,' I said, as Holly's car pulled
up outside. 'Now go on, have a lovely day and I'll be
here waiting to hear all about it when you get back.'

It was nice to have a few hours to myself but I couldn't
help feeling nervous for Elise and praying that her
grandmother actually did have the capacity to forgive
and forget. Hopefully, if this went well, it could be the
first step on the road to a fuller reconciliation, and

perhaps Elise even moving back in with her. She'd grown up so much in the time she'd been with us, and though I had no illusions about the stress involved in taking on a complicated teenager, this was her nan, and this was a blood tie that had already been proven, even if it had ended up being stretched to breaking point. If Elise could just show her how much she had changed, then perhaps Nan would even see it as a blessing to have her teenage granddaughter around the place, especially as she was slightly infirm.

Stop it, I chastised myself. We didn't live in cloud cuckoo land, and I was letting my imagination run away with me. I didn't know the first thing about the woman, after all. Far better to wait and see what transpired at the meeting, and in the meantime forget all about it. So, after I'd done a few chores, I decided to do exactly that. Concentrate on my own life. I checked the time. Lunchtime. The perfect time to call Kieron for a catch-up.

'Come on, then,' I said when he answered. 'Hit me with a wedding update. I haven't heard from you all week and there must be plans afoot, so spill!'

My son laughed. 'You do realise I'm at work, mother,' he huffed. 'And yes, I *know* I'm on my lunchbreak, but I'm with a mate so I can't talk.'

'Oh, Kieron!' I said, exasperated. 'There must be *something* I can do. It's August already, in case you hadn't noticed. Hasn't Lauren said anything yet?'

'Mother, I'm a *man*. Do you really expect me to know anything?' He laughed then. 'Oh, go on, then. I think she's calling you tonight or tomorrow. I think she wants to see when you can get together to talk "wedmin", as she calls it. Satisfied?'

'Satisfied.'

Though, of course, I wasn't, and wouldn't be till I'd had the call from Lauren. And, in the meantime, with nothing calling to me sufficiently strongly to grab my attention, there was nothing for it but to tackle the pile of ironing that had been growing in the conservatory. I couldn't even slope off to visit my parents, as they'd gone on a coach trip with some senior citizen group they had joined – honestly, they had a better social life than I did!

I was almost an hour into it when I finally heard the door go. I rushed into the hall to greet Elise and was almost knocked over as she rushed to greet me.

'Casey! You'll never guess!' she said, once she and Holly were properly inside. 'My nan cried – actually *cried* – when she saw me! Didn't she, Holly? I mean, this is *Nan*. Nan who *never* cries!'

I wasn't sure about that. This might be a nan who would 'batter' any miscreants, but my hunch was that she'd probably shed a fair few tears in the last few months.

'That's great,' I said, hugging her. 'Oh, Elise, I'm so happy for you.'

She looked at Holly then. 'And there's more. Will you tell her or shall I?'

'You, of course,' Holly said. 'It's your news, not mine.'

Casey Watson

It seemed that halfway through the visit, Holly's phone had rang and she'd excused herself to take the call outside. She didn't mention it to Nan or Elise at first as it had been Elise's dad – finally returning Holly's calls. When he heard that Elise was actually there, at his mother's house, he asked if he could say hello, which of course, having checked with Elise, Holly had allowed.

'I mean, timing or what?' Elise beamed. 'Isn't that spooky?'

'It was certainly a happy coincidence,' Holly agreed.

'Because apparently witch-stepmother has agreed that he can talk to me. And here's the best bit, she's even allowing him to *see* me.'

'Really?' I asked, searching Holly's face for clarification. 'That's great news.'

Holly nodded. 'I obviously need to run it by my manager, but yes, it's great, and we should be able to put something in place by next week. The only thing is that it has to be at Grandmother's house. But Mrs Blackwell has said she's more than happy for that to happen, like a joint visit type of thing.'

Elise grabbed my arm, her joy shining from her face. 'Isn't it great, Casey? My dad finally wants to start seeing me. I mean, the witch-stepmother –'

'Perhaps April?'

'Alright, *April*. She won't let it happen at their house, not yet, but I'm not bothered about that. It's not her I want to see. It's Dad, and now I can. Isn't that brilliant?'

Brilliant, but with qualifications and reservations, I thought privately. This could still yet come to nothing, and I so desperately didn't want her hopes raised and then dashed. But I painted on the biggest, brightest smile I could manage and hugged her a second time. 'That's brilliant news, sweetie. I'm over the moon for you, I really am.'

And I was. At least, mostly. Yes, this was great news for Elise, and I could see how excited she was, but the alarm bells were ringing loud and clear in my head. Stepmum had had to sanction this, and she'd obviously made it clear that Elise wasn't allowed in their home. Dad had only stepped up when she'd given the go-ahead, which meant she was still calling the shots. If that was the case – which it clearly was – then she could just as easily pull the carpet from under everybody's feet at any time she chose, and that would be devastating for Elise. So, while I was happy for the girl, who looked fit to burst with happiness, I felt a little sick, too, that her dad hadn't been strong willed enough to make this happen under his own terms.

But it was, as I kept thinking, what it was. Before Holly left, we had a few moments alone, while Elise went upstairs to get changed. She explained that she would be supervising the next visit too – the one to which they could hopefully invite Dad as well. 'But I will come out the day before to see Elise,' she said, 'just so that we can go over a few rules before they all get together and, well,' she nodded upstairs and frowned a little, 'try as much as we can to manage her expectations.'

Which would be hard, I knew, because Cinderella was at last going to the ball. Fingers crossed the dream didn't end at midnight.

Chapter 22

Despite my misgivings about Dad's intentions, I was pleased to see that he at least honoured every single visit that was arranged, albeit still at his mother's house. For the next four weeks, because it was still the summer holidays, every Wednesday, Elise would come downstairs at 10 a.m., hair and make-up done beautifully, and dressed demurely and smartly, all excited to watch out for Holly arriving to take her to her contact. After the first three sessions it had been decided that they no longer needed to be supervised, so Holly would simply pick Elise up and drop her off at Grandma's, and then collect her and bring her home again four hours later, as they'd also increased the length of the visits.

'I think Dad's getting a bit sick of witch-stepmother,' Elise said the following Wednesday morning as she watched out of the window for Holly, 'because last week, when they told us we could start going out places if we liked, he seemed really sad when I said that her kids might want to meet us at the park or something. Then he seemed to get angry – not with me, but over *her*. He said it wouldn't matter if they'd like it or not – and they probably would, he said – but that he had no say in the matter.'

This was all said in such a matter-of-fact way that I knew Elise wasn't that upset about it, but, still, I had to ask.

'Did that hurt you to know that, love?' I asked. 'That she is still controlling such things?'

Elise shrugged. 'Not so much that,' she said, 'but it kind of upsets me that Dad doesn't stand up to her. Honestly, why are men and boys so *weak*? At first, when I lived there, it felt like he was putting them first all the time and that I didn't matter, but now I kind of see things differently. I know that he loves me and wants to make me happy, but he's too weak to fight for it.' She shrugged again. 'I mean, I don't know if that's true, or if I'm just making excuses for him. But that's how it feels to me, anyway.'

'I think you're absolutely right, sweetie,' I said, feeling sad for her. She was showing impressive wisdom and insight beyond her years, but a girl of her age shouldn't have to analyse and justify why her dad did the things he did. She shouldn't be the one waiting for him to man up and do the right thing. It was *very* frustrating. 'But you know, one day things will change. One day he will see what an absolute star you are and he'll regret missing out on the time he could have spent with you, I'm sure of it.'

Elise's eyes lit up at this. 'Thanks, Casey, and God I hope you're right. But for now things are going really well so I don't want to push him and make him feel like he's backed into a corner between me and her. And, you know, my nan said *exactly* what you just said, last week, when he was taking her bins out.' She grinned. 'She said that when I'm not around she gives him what for and she called the witch-stepmother a controlling little cow.'

I laughed. 'You know what?' I said. 'I think me and your nan would get along like a house on fire. Anyway,' I added, nodding towards the window, 'Holly's outside. Better scoot.'

Elise pulled me in for a quick hug. 'You *so* would,' she said.

I suspected she was right. I had a lot of time for Nan. And a much clearer sense now of why she'd acted like she had. Not because she didn't care about Elise, but because she did. And with a hefty dose of self-knowledge, as well. It must have been the hardest thing imaginable to see her granddaughter taken into care, but what other options must she genuinely have considered she had left to her? She was nominally in charge of an off-the-rails fourteen-year-old, hardly seeing her, having no means of controlling or guiding her, and with nothing in the way of a back-up plan. And with no family bar a son who'd already let Elise down badly and was still in a relationship that precluded him from stepping up, what other options *did* she have? None. It was another stark reminder that, for all we imagine otherwise, we are truly lucky if we have a support network around us. I felt clear in my mind now. Elise's gran had done what she thought was the best thing for Elise – instead of repeating the cycle of rebuke and recrimination she had decided to draw the line that, though painful (and I'm sure her guilt must have given her many sleepless nights), would at least give Elise a chance of being helped to sort her life out – via the safety net that local authority care, and a foster family, could provide. And hats off to her, I thought. She'd been right, hadn't she?

But what was going to happen now? Mrs Blackwell wasn't getting any younger (or more sprightly, for that matter, despite the new knee – I'd heard the other one was currently on the waiting list), and the prospect of having her granddaughter back in her life was very different to the prospect of once again being *in loco parentis*.

So, would Elise stay with us for the foreseeable? I turned the idea over in my mind and found it not disagreeable. That hug she'd just given me, for instance – that spoke volumes. As did the fact that in a quiet way – almost by stealth – the girl who had so liked to swim in the shallows, to keep herself to herself, to wear an impenetrable mask, had, almost without us realising it was happening, become embedded in the family. I had long since stopped worrying about what tall tales she'd be telling, or what dramas she'd be involved with; over the six or seven weeks since she'd first bared her soul to me, she'd totally changed her behaviour. She no longer created situations in other people's relationships, and she was spending more time downstairs with me and Mike, rather than hidden away, in her room, on her phone. She was, as the parlance goes, settled.

As things stood, the plan was that Elise would stay with us at least until she turned sixteen, and then, if she wanted to, for us to keep her until she was eighteen. After that the arrangements change in fostering and a child can stay under a loose contract for another couple of years if they wish to, so that they can continue in education or take a job without worrying about supporting themselves. The local authority pay a basic amount to cover their food and utilities, but the child has to either work or go onto benefits and pay an amount to the carer towards their upkeep. They also have to pay for their own phone contracts, their clothes and make-up, etc. It was a good arrangement in my opinion and a lifeline to some kids who would otherwise drop out of the system and then start to drown in reality as they realised that life on the outside was really tough. Of course, some would get through it, some would go off to university or secure themselves a job that paid enough to get by on their own, but a lot didn't, and staying put offered them continued support and security.

I don't often get this feeling, but as I watched Holly's car drive off, I wondered if that's what would happen with Elise. Somehow, I thought not. However much events of the last few weeks had changed her, the past hadn't, and as a result of it she'd become fiercely independent and determined to rely on nobody but herself. And perhaps that was a good thing, as, ultimately, whatever happened with her nan and her father, as an adult she would have to do exactly that.

I was reminded of a time when Riley and Kieron were little and were playing out in the garden together. Riley had suddenly burst in yelling for me to come outside. 'Kieron's crying, Mummy,' she'd shouted. 'It's a bird, a baby bird! And it can't fly, it's hurt!'

I'd rushed out to see, and, as Riley had said, poor Kieron was really sobbing as he cradled the tiny injured bird, who was, I estimated, only recently fledged.

Naturally, Kieron and Riley had wanted to bring it inside, to the warmth of the kitchen, and make a pet of it, but my hunch had been that there would be a better solution – we'd make it a nice warm nest in the shed. 'And every day you can bring it food and water, while it heals. But then, kids,' I explained, 'when it's better, it will, and it must, fly away.'

For the next three days they looked after the little bird as if they were its parents. Then, sure enough, on the fourth day they came down to find it gone. Which upset them, particularly as it hadn't waited so they could say goodbye to it, but after we chatted they accepted it. It was free and it had flown. And, in their children's minds, to find its mum.

This was exactly how I felt right now. Elise had been

our broken bird and we'd tended to her and taken away some of her pain, and now that she felt fixed enough, she was going to flutter off, just like the baby bird had, and seek out, if not her mum, then her place in the world. Which I could only hope would include at least some members of her family. Okay, yes, I was being a bit twee thinking that, and it wasn't as if anyone had yet even discussed the future, but something in me knew that was what was going to happen.

I didn't have much time to dwell on it, however, as later that day I got the call I'd been waiting for from Lauren. Finally! Did she have some sixth sense? (She wasn't up to speed yet on developments, so I figured she must have.) Because, in any event, when was a good time, she asked, for her to come round to ours and start making plans for the wedding?

'Now,' I said. '*Now* is good. Does tonight work for you?'

'Tonight's perfect,' she said. Which was music to my ears. 'Kieron's going to watch the kids,' she said, 'but they'll be in bed anyway, so actually it's just a great excuse for him to play online gaming with a group of his friends, so I thought I'd bring a bottle of wine round. Mike can sit in the front room and watch his cop stuff, and you, me and Elise can get our heads together round the kitchen table.'

'Sounds like a plan,' I said, touched. 'And thanks *so* much for allowing Elise to be involved. She'll be thrilled to be part of it.'

'No worries,' my lovely future daughter-in-law said. 'In fact, I'll make the wine fizzy and bring some fresh orange juice too – that way she can join in with a drink too, if that's okay with you?'

A small Buck's Fizz never harmed anyone of Elise's age – indeed, I often allowed it on Christmas Day – so I was more than happy to agree to this as a one-off.

And, as I suspected, Elise was over the moon to be sitting round the table with us, talking all things wedding, and it seemed she was quite the little organ-iser, chipping in with advice and suggestions.

'Have you thought about making your wedding cake the dessert?' was one of her best ones. 'Specially if you're going for sticky toffee and chocolate brownie layers.'

'Sticky toffee wedding cake?' I said, shocked. 'I thought that was a pudding. Is that a thing now?'

They both nodded. 'A girl at school, her big sister had three layers – sticky toffee, chocolate brownie and lemon drizzle,' Elise explained. 'They served it for dessert with cream or custard.'

'Not a fruit cake?' I asked.

Lauren made a gagging sound. '*No one* likes fruit cake,' she told me.

I gaped. 'No one likes fruit cake?'

'Or marzipan,' said Elise. 'Except old people.'

'You know what?' Lauren said. 'That's a brilliant idea. Who wants piles of leftover cake after a wedding anyway?'

I thought fondly back to the top tier Mike and I had saved for the first christening. How, despite everyone promising it would have 'matured' perfectly, we'd opened the box to find a horrible, mouldy mess. She was right. 'Well, I'll be making a Christmas *fruit* cake anyway,' I said. 'So the old people, as you put it, will be catered for anyway.'

'Exactly,' said Lauren, raising her glass. 'So that's sorted, then!'

I watched as the two of them thrashed out lots of other ideas, blonde heads bent together over the scrapbook, as they went through some of Lauren's more outrageous ideas. And Elise looked like the picture of happiness. Not at all like the broken baby bird I'd had in my head earlier. And I couldn't help but muse on it. It was such a shame that these kids had no say in where they were born, or who they were born to, but our little Cinderella child had come a long way, and I felt very proud of her. I obviously hoped her nan and dad could see what I saw – and then some – but, whatever happened, I had a hunch she would be okay.

Chapter 23

There was only a week and a half left of the summer holidays and I was browsing online for a new blazer and school bag for Elise when I received the call from Christine Bolton. The call that would set the wheels in motion for Elise to move on from us.

'So, great news, Casey, and that makes a welcome change, doesn't it? Perhaps we do live in cloud cuckoo land after all!'

I laughed. 'Depends on what this great news is,' I said, 'so don't keep me in suspense.'

'Mrs Blackwell has put in an application to the courts to have Elise move in with her, permanently. So it looks like there will be a happy ending for the girl after all.'

'That *is* great news,' I said, 'but an application to the courts? Did she have to do that?'

'She did,' Christine said, 'but it's just red tape really, a box-ticking thing. It has to be passed by the judge who ruled originally about Elise being in care, because what she's asking for is for us to continue to be involved – in a much smaller way than we are now, of course, but still there in the background, offering support. So, the application is for Elise to remain in care but with a family member, and we are supporting the motion.'

I knew that this was something the courts preferred to do for a child. It was far better for them to live with someone they knew and who knew them, so I had no doubt this was indeed just a matter of red tape. The judge would almost certainly agree.

'There are a few things that will need ironing out,' Christine continued. 'Just logistics really. But you can tell Elise the news and see how she feels about it, and then Holly will ring her either later today or tomorrow,' Christine said, 'and once that's all done, that will be it.'

'So, how long are we talking?' I asked. 'Days? Weeks?'

'I would say a couple of weeks tops,' she answered. 'It won't be longer than that because of course she will have to get back into her old school or at least a different school, if that one's not an option.'

So at least I wouldn't be forking out a small fortune for a new blazer, then, I told myself as I closed my laptop. I was happy, of course I was. Poor Elise had never felt she belonged anywhere, and now she would know that she was wanted, and that she was back in the fold of the family she loved. But I still felt this nagging doubt, this feeling that there was unfinished business. Still, there was no way I was going to allow this to dampen Elise's happiness, so I did what I always did – made a coffee, took a big slurp and then ran with it up to her room.

'Elise! Guess what?' I said as I knocked and walked into her room.

Elise was on her phone, grinning from ear to ear as she looked at me. 'Nan, I think Casey's just found out,' she said into the phone, laughing. 'I'll call you back, okay? But thanks, Nan. I love you.'

'Oh,' I said, play-acting at looking deflated. 'Well, that's taken the wind out of my sails, then! So, yes,' I added grinning, 'Christine just rang me, and oh, sweetie, I'm *so* happy for you, I really am. I'm guessing I don't need to ask if it's what you want, then?'

'It really is. I don't know whether to laugh or cry I'm so happy!'

'Do both,' I laughed, 'that's what I always do. Oh love, honestly, I'm made up for you.'

Elise grinned. 'Dad knows all about it too, and he's also made up. He told Nan he'll call round all the time when I move in, not just once a week, and he even said that he's going to work on you-know-who, so that I can go round to theirs. It's only a walk away so, if I'm allowed, I'll be able to go round all the time!'

I smiled as she babbled on about how great this all was but I couldn't help thinking she had put her rose-tinted glasses back on. In her head, the future was once again all pink and fluffy, and I didn't want to be the one to shatter her dreams.

'Steady on, Mrs,' I said, trying to keep my tone jovial. 'One step at a time, girl. Get yourself settled back in with your nan first and let Dad's visits build up gradually. No point in rushing things now after all this time, is there? Plenty of time for that, sweetie.'

'You're right,' Elise said. 'I'm doing what I usually do, aren't I? Don't worry, I'll give my head a shake. I don't want to scare Dad off, not when it's all going so well again.'

I smiled at her serious expression. 'I don't think you'll scare him off, Elise – how could anyone be scared of that beautiful face? Now go on, phone your nan back. I know you're excited and I'm sure she's told you it might take a couple of weeks to get all sorted, but I'm sure you have lots to catch up on.'

I went back downstairs and finished my coffee, thinking back on our time with Elise. She really had changed. I knew I'd done my job well as far as that was concerned, so why did I still have this stupid sinking feeling?

'I don't think it's about Elise, love,' Mike said later, when we were in bed. 'I've been thinking about what you said before about unfinished business, and you know, I think you hit the nail on the head. There's a fair few loose ends left untied here – like the other kids, Saffy and baby Dom. We haven't taken Elise to see them yet and that might prove tricky. They could well resent her, at least initially – particularly the girl – for turning their lives upside down. I know it will be driving you crazy not knowing how they're doing, and then there's the mother.

I know you, Case, and it will be unsettling you knowing she's still out there doing her thing and we don't know how the police investigation is going, do we? You're afraid she'll get away scot-free, I know you are.'

It was as if a veil had been lifted from my face. Mike was right and I knew it instantly. For me to feel truly happy about Elise moving on, I had to know all that background stuff, for her sake and for mine. For me, just to satisfy my curiosity, and to know the ending of the full story, but for Elise it was so much more important. I wanted her to leave us without having to lock away any unanswered questions, without worrying about the family that she *didn't* see. I knew then that I had to try and sort this out.

Over the next couple of days, while Elise was busy phoning around the friends she had made at school, telling them that she wouldn't be going back, I was busy making arrangements with Christine Bolton and Holly for taking Elise across the county to visit with her younger siblings. Saffy and Dom's foster carers were more than happy to facilitate this and wanted to be the ones to surprise me with the news that they were going through the process of adopting the children. I was thrilled – there really couldn't have been a better outcome for them – and when they phoned me to invite us down two days later Elise was ecstatic.

'Oh my God, Casey! That's just fantastic!' she said. 'I'm so happy for them, so happy they won't ever have to live that life anymore. I can't wait to see them.'

She didn't have to wait for long, although I wouldn't be part of it. I now had to take a back seat in all of Elise's plans for the future and I fully understood that. Holly came to take her to see them, and although Elise wanted me to accompany them, she accepted it when I explained that this was a moment just for her and the children, and that she could tell me all about it when she came home.

I used the time I had alone to do some investigative work about what was happening with Kennedy. I wanted to be able to set Elise's mind at rest about the matter and have her not worry about the woman turning up and blaming her for the children being taken. That was my greatest fear; that somehow Elise would try to shoulder that blame if her mother got to her after she left us. I wanted to ensure I'd done all I could to prevent this from happening.

I said as much to Christine when she called me. 'Well, you don't need to worry about Uncle Max at least,' she told me. 'I've just heard he's been charged and he's also been refused bail. His trial is set for next year but the fact they've kept him in says it all, and from what we've been told he is expecting a long sentence. There were, sad to say, several other children involved.'

'But the mother,' I pressed, 'will she go to prison too? Surely she'll be punished. She was part of it all, she *knew*!'

'I don't think she will,' Christine said, sadly. 'It's terrible really, but Max refused to give evidence against her. She swore she knew nothing about it, and, in her defence, the abuse of her own children did seem to happen when she was out working.' She sighed. 'Well, if you can call it that. But even though both girls said they told mum, she is categorically denying it. She's accepted she was a rotten mother and has freely given up all parental responsibility for all of them, and she has accepted the judge's order that she has no contact whatsoever with them.'

'And that's it, then?' I asked, bewildered. 'No bloody punishment whatsoever?'

'She's been ordered to attend rehab and is on a conditional discharge,' Christine said, her voice flat. I knew she was as disheartened as I was.

'Great!' I said, sighing. 'Well, I suppose I should be thankful for the conditional discharge. At least now if she contacts any of them she will be in breach and could end up in prison in the long run.'

'Exactly,' Christine said. 'At least there's that, so we must be thankful. Are you going to tell Elise if she asks?'

'I'm going to tell her either way,' I said. 'She deserves to know and it might put her mind at rest. It will be up to her then to ensure she doesn't add her on anything and to be strong enough to not initiate any future contact. Though I don't think she will now, do you?'

Christine didn't, and she agreed with what I intended to do. So that was it. All my loose ends were tied up now – or at least as much as they could be. All that remained now was to wait for the date from the courts to say when Elise could move back in with her grand-mother.

That date came through quicker than we were prepared for so, a little less than a week since Christine first called me about it, Mike – who had of course taken the morning off – Elise and myself were sitting in the living room sipping coffee and chatting about everything other than the elephant in the room. That being the two huge pink suitcases propped up by the sofa. The two cases I'd only bought yesterday and which were now filled with all of Elise's belongings.

'Cheer up, Casey,' Elise said as she put her mug down on the side table. 'Tyler said you'd be all sad and soppy this morning.' She grinned at me. 'I FaceTimed him after breakfast because he made me promise to. He said he wouldn't go to work until I had, and he said I had to tell you not to cry.'

'Me, *cry*?' I said, also laughing. My son knew me so well. 'As if. Hard as nails, me. I'm just sad that you're taking those gorgeous cases – I wanted them for Tenerife.'

'Tenerife? You're going off on holiday the minute I'm out of the door? Charming!'

I shook my head. 'Nope, silly. Not till after Kieron and Lauren's wedding. And that's between the three of us. I haven't told anybody yet.'

Mike rolled his eyes. 'I think you're getting mixed up in your old age, Case. It's the bride and groom that have a honeymoon, not the bloody mum and dad!'

'Whatever, Mike,' I said, waving my arm dramatically in front of my face.

Holly arrived before Mike could find out if I was serious or not. In fact, I was – not about the cases; I'd bought them for Elise – but because I knew after the wedding I'd be plunged into gloom. I hated January at the best of times, but after the excitement of the wedding, I saw it as an insurance policy against getting the glums. But I'd work on Mike later; right now we had another foster child to send off and, within minutes, we were hauling the pink suitcases into the boot of Holly's car. And I was crying. Of course I was. The amount of times I'd done this, but I *still* couldn't control myself!

'We're going to miss you so much, love,' I told Elise, furiously wiping away my tears. 'I'm sorry to blubber, but please, please stay in touch, won't you?'

Elise hugged me tightly, and I felt her tears mingling with my own. 'When I think of what I put you guys through in the beginning,' she said, 'I'm so sorry for that. *So* sorry.'

She frowned then and fell silent. 'What?' I said. 'Spill!'

'It's just Jan. I feel so terrible. Will you let her know I'm sorry? I'm going to write to her, but will you tell her too? It was an awful thing I did, saying all those things I did about her. I just didn't want to go back there. Not once I came to you. And it wasn't anything to do with her – *or* you and Mike – I just wanted to be back in town. Because she lived out in the sticks ... I mean, it really was miles from anywhere ... and I just thought if I – oh God, Casey, I really feel *so* awful. I don't know what possessed me. I just –'

I took her hands in my own. 'Love, I *know*. And so does Jan. And I'll pass on your apology. She'll be really glad to know that. And to get a letter from you too. That will really mean a lot to her. But it's done now. Line drawn. So, don't dwell on it, okay? It's all about the future now. *Your* future.'

She nodded tearfully. 'And of course I'll stay in touch. Just try to stop me. You'll be sick of hearing from me!'

'No way,' I said as I pulled away and opened the car door for her. 'It's not really the done thing, but I'll add you on Facebook. I don't do that tick-clock thingy, or anything else, really, but I do do Facebook, so accept me and we can chat all the time.'

Elise laughed and glanced at Holly. 'Tick-clock thingy? Get me away from this mad woman!'

And then they were gone. And as we watched them go, I felt Mike's arm snake around my shoulder. 'Smile, love,' he said, squeezing my arm. 'Keep smiling. You can do the whole snivelling and sobbing bit once they're gone.'

'Oh, stop it!' I said, play-punching him in the side. 'You're heartless, you are. Anyway, I can't help it. It's just the bloody menopause.'

'*Really*?' he said. 'Well, I'm no doctor but if it is, you should definitely see someone, I reckon. Because, by my calculation, you've been menopausal for at *least* twenty years. Which makes you a mystery to all of modern medical science.'

For which he got another punch.

Honestly, men!

Epilogue

A few days after Elise moved out, she actually started to have cold feet. She was happy back at her nan's, but she was also very anxious – being back living in the old neighbourhood and seeing the friends she used to hang around with, she began to worry that she could easily revert back to her old self. So, desperately anxious not to mess up, she called and asked me to ask Christine if I could be allowed to keep her placement open for a month after she left, just in case.

I understood where she was coming from – she just needed that safety blanket. But I had no such worries; Elise was a completely different person now. But both Christine and her manager agreed that this would be fine. Of course, it meant that I wouldn't be taking any other children in for that month, but, given the timing, I didn't mind that at all. It meant I had the time to go all out for my own family. I spent time in York with Ty and Naomi for a bit, helped Riley redecorate her kitchen and, best of all, went shopping with Lauren for a beautiful mother of the groom outfit. (One that didn't clash with her mum's – we both chose different shades of blue.)

As I suspected, though, Elise didn't need that month. She settled down just fine at her grandmother's and told me, via one of our regular chats on Messenger, that she was the happiest she had been in years. Her dad had increased his visits to twice weekly and he often took Elise out for a meal or to the local bowling alley, which she loved.

I so loved hearing about how Elise was loving life finally. She was attending a completely new school and had caught up on her education; in fact she was excelling in her favourite subjects, English and Geography.

The very best news, however, came about three months after she'd left us. Dad had finally stepped up and had a huge row with the 'witch-stepmother', demanding that his only real daughter be allowed to be part of his everyday life and that meant coming to the family home. His wife, however, wouldn't have it and it took its toll on what had turned out to be an already troubled marriage. In the end, one night, after yet another blazing row, she apparently packed up all her things, gathered up her two children and left the house, saying she wanted a divorce.

Rather than uproot and disrupt any more lives, Elise's father had insisted his wife and her children remain in their home until the kids were old enough to leave school, and he moved in with his mother and Elise. Of course, Elise was over the moon about this and so was her nan, who had been trying for months to get her son to stand up for what was right. I was delighted, and though I felt a little bit sorry for the family he had left behind, I had no such feelings for the stepmother. She'd had every opportunity to do right by Elise and, as far as I could see, she never had.

Now, a few years down the line, Elise has a boyfriend – and I'm glad to report, one closer to her own age. She met him soon after leaving school, when she went to college to train to become a travel agent. Alex was at the same one, a year into a chef's course. It was, apparently, love at first sight, and Elise says he is definitely 'the one'.

'The one' or not, I couldn't be prouder of Elise. Against all odds, our little broken bird has found her own nest and her wings, and I can't wait to find out how far she can fly.

CASEY WATSON

One woman determined to make a difference.

Read Casey's poignant memoirs and be inspired.

MUMMY, PLEASE DON'T LEAVE

When baby Tommy – born in prison – and
his half-brother, Seth, are placed in The Watsons'
care, their troubled teenage mother soon
follows suit.

Casey is determined to keep this family together,
but her confidence falters. Can she find the energy
and strength to see this unusual case through?

LET ME GO

Harley is an anxious teen who wants to end her own life, and there's only one woman who can find out why

Casey makes a breakthrough which sheds light on the disturbing truth – there is a man in Harley's life, a very dangerous man indeed.

A DARK SECRET

A troubled nine-year-old with a violent streak, Sam's relentless bullying sees even his siblings beg not to be placed with him

When Casey delves into Sam's past she uncovers something far darker than she had imagined.

A BOY WITHOUT HOPE

A history of abuse and neglect has left Miller destined for life's scrap heap

Miller's destructive behaviour will push Casey to her limits, but she is determined to help him overcome his demons and give him hope.

NOWHERE TO GO

Eleven-year-old Tyler has stabbed his stepmother and has nowhere to go

With his birth mother dead and a father who doesn't want him, what can be done to stop his young life spiralling out of control?

GROOMED

Keeley is urgently rehomed with Casey after accusing her foster father of abuse

It's Casey's job to keep Keeley safe, but can she protect this strong-willed teen from the dangers online?

THE SILENT WITNESS

Bella's father is on a ventilator, fighting for his life, while her mother is currently on remand in prison, charged with his attempted murder

Bella is the only witness.

RUNAWAY GIRL

Adrianna arrives on Casey's doorstep with no possessions, no English and no explanation

It will be a few weeks before Casey starts getting the shocking answers to her questions . . .

MUMMY'S LITTLE SOLDIER

Leo isn't a bad lad, but his frequent absences from school mean he's on the brink of permanent exclusion

Leo is clearly hiding something, and Casey knows that if he is to have any kind of future, it's up to her to find out the truth.

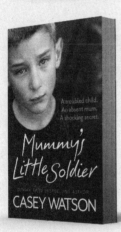

SKIN DEEP

Flip is being raised by her alcoholic mother, and comes to Casey after a fire at their home

Flip has Foetal Alcohol Syndrome (FAS), but it soon turns out that this is just the tip of the iceberg . . .

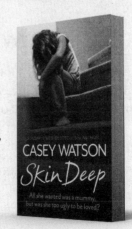

A STOLEN CHILDHOOD

Kiara appears tired and distressed, and the school wants Casey to take her under her wing for a while

On the surface, everything points to a child who is upset that her parents have separated. The horrific truth, however, shocks Casey to the core.

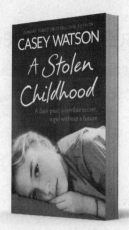

THE GIRL WITHOUT A VOICE

What is the secret behind Imogen's silence?

Discover the shocking and devastating past of a child with severe behavioural problems.

A LAST KISS FOR MUMMY

A teenage mother and baby in need of a loving home

At fourteen, Emma is just a child herself – and one who's never been properly mothered.

BREAKING THE SILENCE

Two boys with an unlikely bond

With Georgie and Jenson, Casey is facing her toughest test yet.

MUMMY'S LITTLE HELPER

A young girl secretly caring for her mother

Abigail has been dealing with pressures no child should face. Casey has the difficult challenge of helping her to learn to let go.

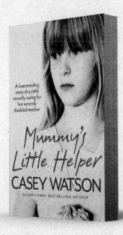

TOO HURT TO STAY

Branded 'vicious and evil', eight-year-old Spencer asks to be taken into care

Casey and her family are disgusted: kids aren't born evil. Despite the challenges Spencer brings, they are determined to help him find a loving home.

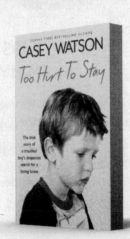

LITTLE PRISONERS

Abused siblings who do not know what it means to be loved

With new-found security and trust, Casey helps Ashton and Olivia to rebuild their lives

CRYING FOR HELP

A damaged girl haunted by her past

Sophia pushes Casey to the limits, threatening the safety of the whole family. Can Casey make a difference in time?

THE BOY NO ONE LOVED

Five-year-old Justin was desperate and helpless

Six years after being taken into care, Justin has had 20 failed placements. Casey and her family are his last hope.

TITLES AVAILABLE AS E-BOOK ONLY

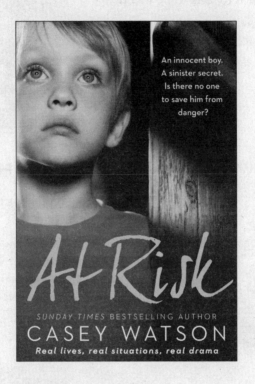

AT RISK

Adam is brought to Casey while his mum
recovers in hospital – just for a few days

But a chance discovery reveals that Casey has stumbled upon
something altogether more sinister . . .

THE LITTLE PRINCESS

Six-year-old Darby is naturally distressed at being removed from her parents just before Christmas

And when the shocking and sickening reason is revealed, a Happy New Year seems an impossible dream as well . . .

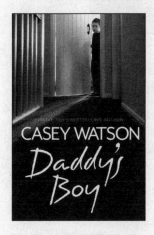

DADDY'S BOY

Paulie, just five, is a boy out of control – or is he just misunderstood?

The plan for Paulie is simple: get him back home with his family. But perhaps 'home' isn't the best place for him . . .

THE WILD CHILD

Angry and hurting, eight-year-old Connor is from a broken home

As streetwise as they come, he's determined to cause trouble. But Casey is convinced there is a frightened child beneath the swagger.

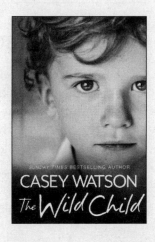

NO PLACE FOR NATHAN

Nathan has a sometime alter ego called Jenny who is the only one who knows the secrets of his disturbed past

But where is Jenny when she is most needed?

SCARLETT'S SECRET

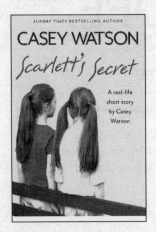

Jade and Scarlett, seventeen-year-old twins, share a terrible secret

Can Casey help them come to terms with the truth and rediscover their sibling connection?

JUST A BOY

Cameron is a sweet boy who seems happy in his skin – making him rather different from most of the other children Casey has cared for

But what happens when Cameron disappears? Will Casey's worst fears be realised?